QUEEN MAUD LAND

To our very dear Uncle Magnar

As manager of Ekspertkjeden, you were an unfailing support for the Five Summits expedition and Dronning Maud Land 1994. Sadly you were taken from us one Sunday afternoon in September, and never got to take part in our adventures.

THE BEST

Death is as summer lightning;
    clearly we see, and sigh
for every life in its pure white pain:
        It is the best who die.

Is not each one who has known them
        richer for death's blessed fire -
for men have valued their friendship
    and children have called them sire

They enhanced the life they departed.
    In other men's hearts they lie.
On their headstones it shall be written:
        The best of us never die.

Nordahl Grieg

I would like to thank all members of the expedition for a fantastic experience and a memory for life. Thank you for having helped in the preparation of this book with articles, photos, diary entries, paintings, criticism and enthusiasm.

I am especially grateful to my father and Thomas. Without their help, I could never have gone on the expedition.

Thanks to Susan, Trond, Sigurd, Jan and Bjørn of the Norwegian Polar Institute for expert knowledge, proof reading, and support for the expedition both before and afterwards. Thanks to David for his great commitment to the expedition and the book.

Special thanks to Tina. Without her, this book would never have been what I wanted it to be.

Special thanks to Roland Huntford who made it possible to publish this book in English.

Queen Maud Land

IVAR ERIK TOLLEFSEN

'To this day you can still hear people asking: what is the point of all these expeditions? What earthly use are they? Small minds, I always tell myself, have only time for thoughts of bread and butter.'

Roald Amundsen, 1912.

Copyright © Ivar Erik Tollefsen 1994

Paintings, cartoons and other illustrations: Vebjørn Sand

Maps: Norwegian Polar Institute

Colour separation: Repro-design AS, Oslo.

Binding: Refsum Bokbinderi, Oslo.

Printed by Østlands-Postens press, Larvik

Sales and marketing in Norway: Hjemmet Mortensen Bokforlag AS

Paper: Multiart Gloss 150g. from Carl Emil AS, chlorine-free and environmentally sound. ◍

Cover, layout and graphic design:

   Ivar Erik Tollefsen and Tina Jørgensen of Skaara Design.

Front Cover: Ivar Tollefsen on the north west wall of Ulvetanna - 'The Wolf's Fang'

Insets: Ulvetanna from the south west, penguins on Princess Astrid Coast, skiing up Fenristunga with

Holtanna in the background, Vebjørn Sand on the ice north of Ulvetanna.

'Ulvetanna', litography from Vebjørn Sand's graphic collection from Queen Maud Land.

Page 1: The Ice Queen

Pages 2-3: Ulvetanna and Hel, Fenriskjeften

Page 4-5: Unnamed nunatak west of Fenriskjeften

Page 6-7: Jøkulkyrkja from the north west wall of Ulvetanna

Pages 9-10: Map based on topographical material from the Norwegian Polar Institute.

Page 12: Scanfoto.

Pages 13-17: Lent by the Norwegian Polar Institute. Copyright, Norwegian Polar Institute.

Pages 18-19: Aerial photograph of Fenriskjeften taken in 1959, which Sigurd G. Helle showed me during

the autumn of 1991. Photograph: Norwegian Polar Institute, section of DML 58-59 2038.

Pages 20-21: A few meters below the summit of Ulvetanna.

Page 22: Photograph of Vebjørn Sand by Jørn H.Moen of Dagbladet.

Page 24: Photograph of Boris Yeltsin, Scanfoto.

pp.68-69: Fenriskjeften. Montage and retouching by Piece of Cake AS. Based on two aerial photographs

from the Norwegian Polar Institute, DML 58-59 2014 and 2015. Copyright in the origina photographs

from the Norwegian Polar Institute.

All other photographs in this book were taken by members of the expedition, using Kodak film

(Panther Professional) and mainly Canon cameras.

Contents

MAP 8

A HISTORIC OPPORTUNITY - FOREWORD by Carl Emil Petersen 10

HISTORICAL REVIEW 12

INTRODUCTION - THE DREAM OF QUEEN MAUD LAND 18

13 - A LUCKY NUMBER! 20

A RUSSIAN CHRISTMAS 26

PRINCESS ASTRID COAST 32

THE FIRST ASCENT OF THE HIGHEST MOUNTAIN IN NORWAY 40

ULVETANNA BASE CAMP 50

THE FANGS OF THE WOLF 60

THE FIRST ASCENT OF ULVETANNA - TOPO AND CLIMBING GLOSSARY ... 70

THE NORTH WALL 72

"THE MOST IMPRESSIVE MOUNTAIN I HAVE EVER SEEN" 82

THE CHAMBERMAID 91

A TEMPERAMENTAL LADY 98

A HOLE IN THE TOOTH 108

'DOWN AGAIN AND STILL ALIVE!" 120

HOMEWARD BOUND 128

THE SKIING PARTY'S STORY by Jo Toftdahl 136

IN THE LAND OF THE CAIRN BUILDERS 148

POSTSCRIPT by Vebjørn Sand 156

ACKNOWLEDGEMENTS 158

FAREWELL 160

Jøkulkyrkja *('The Glacier Church')*

Jøkulkyrkja, shining crystal blue
In wilderness of ice and snow
A prize awaiting Norsemen true
A trophy in the morning's glow
Restive, she waits, the men draw near
Climbers who show respect, not fear
Climbers who go where none have gone
With pure Antarctica at one
Gliding on skis with goal in sight
A Cathedral in the polar night

Telegram from my mother and my brother, Terje, New Year's Eve 1993

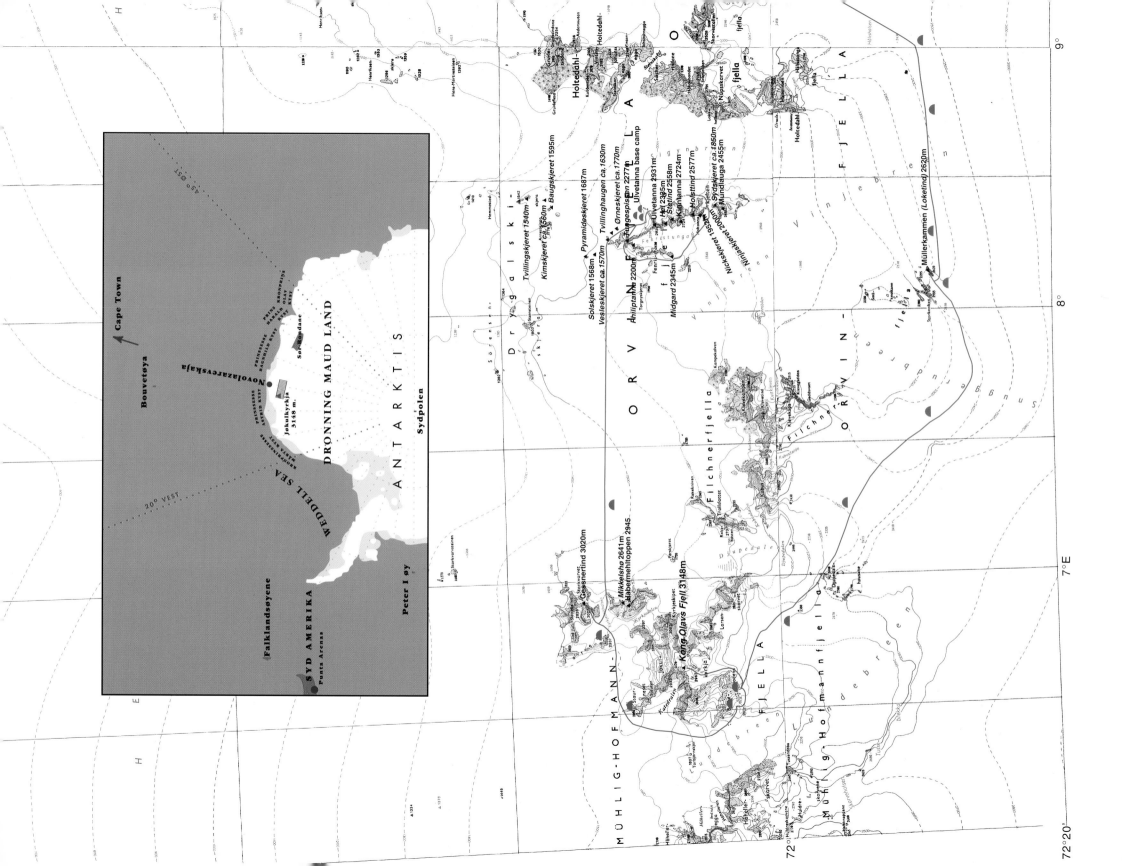

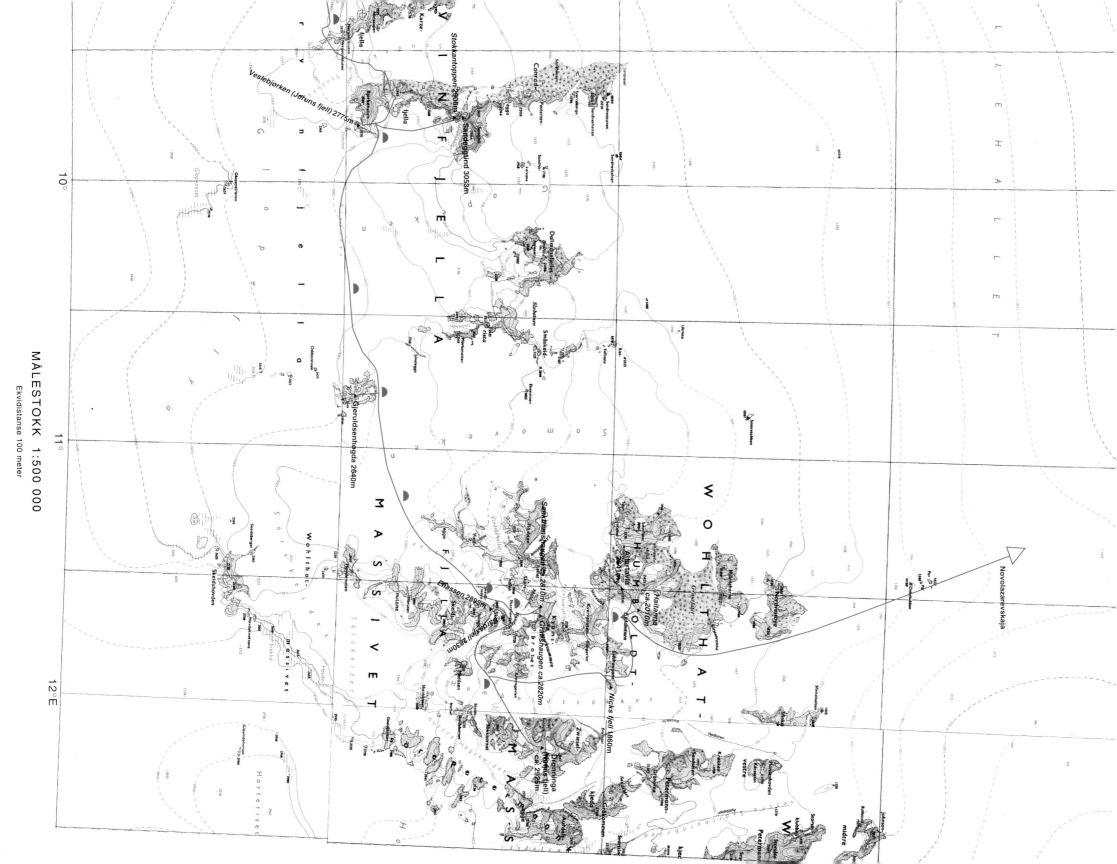

MÅLESTOKK 1:500 000

Ekvidistanse 100 meter

A Historic Opportunity

Antarctica is our fifth largest continent, more than double the size of Australia. It is an island continent, east of the sun, west of the moon and south of everything else. It is covered by an ice cap whose size is such that the sheer figures are hard to grasp: thirty million cubic kilometres of solid ice, so heavy that the part of the underlying land is forced down below sea level.

Radio echo-soundings have shown that the land beneath the ice resembles Norway's deep fjords and narrow valleys. If the ice were to melt, the oceans would rise by 180 feet. More than two thirds of the world's fresh water is locked up in the ice of Antarctica.

Antarctica is also unquestionably the world's highest, most arid, windswept and coldest continent, with a barely credible low temperature record of 89.7 degrees below zero. The Pole itself has six months' sunshine and six months' darkness - with only one sunrise and one sunset every year. Rising at the southern vernal equinox (23. September), the sun steadily spirals upwards to its culmination at the summer solstice (22. December), then sinks in a downward spiral to set at the autumnal equinox (21. March).

To the adventurer and explorer, Antarctica has an even more exciting attribute; it is the least known and most inaccessible of all the continents. In fact it is the only continent free of regular traffic, and the only one where there literally remain large blank white spaces on the map.

Down the centuries, this harsh continent has attracted men of many kinds: explorers, adventurers, sealers, whalers and scientists, but all sharing the same characteristic: they were prepared to face all kinds of danger in their attempts to uncover its secrets. Deep cold, pack ice, storms, scurvy and the polar night have acted like a magnet. Antarctica's very inaccessibility has been an enticement rather than a limitation.

Even on this remote continent, with its vast swathes of unexplored terrain, Queen Maud Land, Norway's Antarctic dependency, emerges as one of the least known regions. Admittedly, most of it was surveyed and photographed from the air some thirty five years ago, but pictures taken from high up and far away can never do justice to this sequestered and majestic mountain kingdom. It is different from most other places in Antarctica. In fact, there is nothing quite like it anywhere else on earth. It is a mountain range half-drowned in a frozen sea, with only the peaks protruding, like islands in an archipelago. Huge monoliths rise up from the surface. The combination of massive vertical rock walls and free-standing summits can probably only be found down there.

Queen Maud Land has existed for millions of years. So has Norway's Highest Mountain, Jøkulkyrkja, and Ulvetanna, and all the other colossi of rock. Although photographs have been available for the last thirty five years, nobody showed any interest until Ivar Tollefsen parked his car outside the Norwegian Polar Institute in the autumn of 1991. The previous spring he and three others had crossed the Greenland ice cap in the shortest time ever recorded (12 days and twenty-three hours), and at this point his hands were full with preparations for the Five of the Seven Summits expedition. Nonetheless he promptly decided to make for Queen Maud Land as soon as that expedition was finished. The Polar Institute, not to mention most other experts, objected that an expedition to this part of Antarctica would be a particularly expensive and complicated affair. This only served to fire his imagination even more. Ivar was familiar with Nansen's words: 'Nothing is impossible, the impossible just takes a little longer.'

This book about Queen Maud Land represents an important and historic contribution to our knowledge of this distant region of the southern hemisphere. The story ranges from a young man's dream of going where no man had been before, via the history of Antarctica, penguins, and icebergs around the ice shelf, to the first ascent of Norway's highest summit, and finally the climbing of Ulvetanna, probably the most difficult mountain, not only in Queen Maud Land, but in the whole of Antarctica. Ivar was not the expedition's most accomplished climber, but it is characteristic of his willpower and determination, that he was one of the trio which reached the top, after nine consecutive days of climbing.

I myself was bitten by the polar bug as far back as 1971, and ever since have felt a strong attraction to the kingdoms of inaccessibility, both north and south. Ivar took me to a continent I had long wanted to see, although I am neither a mountaineer nor exactly young any longer. I was one of a group, thirteen strong, that took part in the first ascent of Norway's Highest Mountain. I experienced dedicated enthusiasm coupled with driving ambition and energy, which both impressed and inspired me. A week's skiing from Jøkulkykkja to Ulvetanna, across a magnificent landscape in the company of new-found friends was adventure indeed. Here we crossed no old ski tracks.

On my daily ski tours out from Base Camp, round Fenriskjeften, or across the snow-bound uplands to Arnesteinen, I was skiing in either ear-shattering silence, or with the sough of icy winds through my snow goggles. Dazzling whiteness, total life-lessness and purity are the impress-ions with which I have been left. If I crossed any tracks then they were my own. I also came into close contact with exhilarating and awe-inspiring climbing. While I was out skiing, my friends would be hanging hundreds of feet up, locked in physical and men-tal battle with the forces of gravity. I felt an intense pleasure merely in being present.

Between the thirteen members of our party, of widely differing backgrounds, ranging in age from 22 to 68, there arose a close friendship and mutual respect. This certainly gave the lie to the maxim of the Norwegian explorer, John Giæver: 'Two men is ideal. Three is one too many. Ten men is hell.' For us, thirteen turned out to be a lucky number.

With a long, happy and adventurous life behind me, I venture to declare unequivocally that I have never experienced anything so wild, so majestic and so unspoiled anywhere else in the world. Queen Maud Land was for me a historic opportunity to be first; not first alone (like my crossing of greenland in 1983), or the first unsupported, or any other contrived variation, but first in the full sense of the word: first to set foot on this wonderful piece of Norway, and first to the top of Norway's Highest Mountain. Humility is the best word to express what I felt - and still feel.

Pål Emil Pedersen

Mellomnes Farm, September 1994.

The Postmaster at Ulvetanna Base Camp.

The Norwegian Post Office rarely gives official status, with a special postmark, to an expedition like ours. Queen Maud Land '94 was authorized to run its own small 'post office' at Ulvetanna Base Camp.

Historical Review

'The Earth is flat,' people said in the days of Homer (800 B.C.), but 300 years later, the Greek philosopher, Pythagoras concluded that the Earth must be round if it were to maintain its equilibrium. One of the Greek names for the north was derived from arctos or bear, to signify the regions under the constellation of the Great Bear; hence our word arctic. Antarctic comes from another ancient Greek word simply meaning 'opposite the bear', possibly coined to express Aristotle's theory of a southern frigid zone to match that of the north.

Between the fifteenth and the eighteenth centuries, the great seafarers; Bartolemeo Diaz, Vasco da Gama, Ferdinand Magellan, Sir Francis Drake, successively helped to show that if a southern continent did indeed exist, it could not be connected with any other land. The final proof of the insularity of Antarctica came with Captain James Cook's circumnavigation of the globe at high latitudes between 1772-75. On 17 January 1773 his ships, Adventure and Resolution, crossed the Antarctic Circle, the very first to do so. Circumstances, however, prevented Cook from actually making a landfall, so a southern continent remained in the realm of myth.

After Cook's death in Hawaii in 1778, nearly forty years went by before a Russian; or to be precise, an Estonian navigator, Vice Admiral Baron Thaddeus von Bellingshausen, on 27 January 1820, arguably became the first man to sight the Antarctic continent. Not that he realized it himself; he thought he saw an iceberg. His ships, 'Mirny' (Peaceful) and 'Vostok' (East) were later commemorated in the names of two Russian bases in the Antarctic. A third base is called after Bellingshausen, and a fourth after his second-in-command, Lazarev (Novolazarevskaya).

In February 1823, a Scottish sealing captain, James Weddell, with two small ships, 'Jane' and 'Beaufoy' reached the 74th parallel, the furthest South so far. Open waters continued to sweep on southwards, but with winter approaching, and men and ships to consider, he decided to turn back. Having sailed so far without seeing land, Weddell concluded that any terra firma round the Pole must be small. As it turned out, he was wrong. Weddell had sailed into one of the two great bights in the coast of Antarctica. It is the one known today as the Weddell Sea.

Even although the ancient Greek philosophers had postulated the existence of a southern continent, during the early part of the nineteenth century, there were few who actually believed in it. Exactly who was the first to sight continental land remains a matter of debate. What is certain is this. In January 1841, an English naval officer, James Clark Ross, with two ships, 'Erebus' and 'Terror' sailed through a belt of pack ice and ran into the open waters of the other great Antarctic bight, now called the Ross Sea. In the space of six weeks, Ross discovered and charted five hundred miles of coastline. He also uncovered a new phenomenon; the Antarctic ice shelf, finding one which now bears his name. Ross also sighted a quiescent volcano, calling it Erebus, after his ship. Ross has always been considered one of the great Antarctic explorers, not only on account of his discoveries, but because when he returned to England in 1843, after an absence of nearly four years, he had accomplished one of the heroic voyages in the annals of the sea. Above all, he had brought back the first clear testimony for the existence of an Antarctic continent.

By 1790 the Americans had established a seal fishery on the island of South Georgia and for most of the nineteenth century, whaling and sealing were the driving force behind Antarctic

Queen Maud

Roald Amundsen made history when he reached the South Pole on 14 December 1911, together with his fellow Norwegians, Helmer Hanssen, Oscar Wisting, Olav Bjaaland and Sverre Hassel.

discovery. Many expeditions were whaling or sealing cruises with exploration as a by-product. In 1892, C.A. Larsen, a redoubtable Norwegian whaling captain with scientific tastes, sailed in 'Jason' into the Weddell Sea. He sighted King Oscar II Land, the first major Antarctic discovery for half a century. Larsen went ashore on Seymour Isle, off the tip of the Antarctic Peninsula. There, he found fossilised traces of vegetation, thus proving that in a past epoch, the climate of Antarctic must have been warmer. (On that voyage, incidentally, Larsen also became the first man known to have used skis in the Antarctic.)

On 24 January 1895 three Norwegians, H.J. Bull, Leonard Kristensen and Carsten Egeberg Borchgrevink, from a whaler called 'Antarktik' went ashore at Cape Adare. At the time, that made them the first men to land on the Antarctic continent. Subsequent historical research has made that claim a matter of debate. But about the sequel there can scarcely be any doubt. In 1899, Borchgrevink returned to Cape Adare and made the historic first wintering on the Antarctic continent. Amongst other things, Borchgrevink and his companions investigated terrestrial magnetism in an attempt to fix precisely the position of the South Magnetic Pole. This was vital for navigating at high latitudes. It was Borchgrevink's great service however, to shift attention from the waters round Antarctica to the continent itself.

In the years that followed, various expeditions penetrated the Ross Ice Shelf, finally reaching the continental ice cap. Meanwhile, in 1908, a party from Shackleton's 'Nimrod' expedition, climbed Mount Erebus (11,382 ft above sea level). This was the first ascent of a major Antarctic peak. But the man who really made history by what he did on Antarctic terra firma was Roald Amundsen. On 14 December 1911, together with Helmer Hanssen, Oscar Wisting, Olav Bjaaland and Sverre Hassel, he reached the South Pole. For several days, Amundsen remained there, meticulously taking observations and criss-crossing the area on skis to make absolutely certain of his goal. Technically, he reached the pole point itself on 17 December. On the way up to the polar plateau, Amundsen passed a mountain range he named after Queen Maud, the Norwegian Queen Consort at the time. The surroundings of the Pole itself, Amundsen called Haakon VII's Plateau, after the reigning Norwegian king. Since the region that we know

Hjalmar Riiser Larsen in his seaplane with 'Norvegia' in the background. In rough seas he had to wait until the plane reached the crest of a wave, before opening the throttle and running along the top of the wave until becoming airborne.

today as Queen Maud Land reaches all the way to the Pole, Amundsen and his men were the first to set foot on what many years later became the Norwegian territorial claim in Antarctica.

As all the world knows, the attainment of the South Pole was in reality a race. Scott was the loser, arriving a month after Amundsen, and perished on the return journey. Amundsen was unaware of this when he left Antarctica in all haste and sailed for Hobart, Tasmania, which he reached on 7 March 1912. Having burned his fingers after his navigation of the North West Passage, when the news leaked out, with heavy financial loss, Amundsen prohibited his men from landing before the news of the attainment of the South Pole appeared in those newspapers to which he was bound by contract.

While Amundsen was celebrating his success, six surviving members of Scott's expedition were going through one of the harshest winters in the history of Antarctic exploration. When their relief ship failed to reach the coast, they spent six months in a snow cave, with seals and penguins their only food. Outside the winter storms raged with temperatures down to sixty degrees of frost.

Even although the Scot, William Spiers Bruce, was the first to reach the coast of Queen Maud Land in 1904 (Bellingshausen was off the coast in 1820), it was the Norwegian whaling shipowner, Lars Christensen, with his several expeditions, who paved the way for Norway's annexation of Queen Maud Land. Christensen dispatched his first expedition as early as 1927, and thereafter in the years leading up to the outbreak of the Second World War, spent huge sums of money on Antarctic exploration. He paid for nine expeditions with the ships Odd, the Norvegia and the Torshavn. He himself sailed with the last four expeditions and on his death in 1967 it was acknowledged that he had done much for the expansion of his country. To secure the whaling industry, Bouvetøya and Peter I's Island were placed under Norwegian sovereignty.

The Norwegian flying pioneers, Hjalmar Riiser-Larsen and Finn Lützow-Holm were a part of the third 'Norvegia' expedition (1929-1930), and from the air they discovered the region now known as Crown Prince Olav's Coast (then Queen Maud Land). A year later they discovered

Princess Ragnhild Coast, and claimed sovereignty by dropping a Norwegian flag at the western extremity of their flight. In 1933 Riiser-Larsen and two others planned a sledging expedition of several thousand kilometres to include all of Norway's possessions in the Antarctic. The day after they were put ashore (as they thought), a tremendous storm blew up. Dogs and supplies ended up scattered around on floes as the ice broke up into smaller and smaller pieces. Eventually they were rescued by the whaler 'Globe'; just in time, as it turned out.

Another Norwegian flying pioneer, Wiggo Widerøe, with his photographer, Nils Romnæs, was the first to sight the mountain massifs within the Norwegian Antarctic sector. Once again it was a private expedition financed by Christensen. From the tanker 'Torshavn', Widerø flew out and photographed parts of Queen Maud Land from the air. The area they were covering stretched from 20° to 80° East longitude.

In 1938 the Germans secretly mounted an expedition to the Antarctic on the orders of Hermann Göring. Together with a ship called 'Schwabenland' were two Dornier aircraft which could be catapulted from the deck to land in the sea and later be hoisted on board again. The Germans' motives were the same as Christensen's for Norway; whaling rights had to be established by material presence and annexation. German international lawyers argued that new territory had to be occupied or marked in some way or other. Tests in the Alps had shown that heavy dart-like projectiles penetrated at least 30 centimetres into the ice when dropped

from an aircraft. While the aircraft photographed new land, they were also to drop these devices engraved with the Nazi swastika.

Whilst these preparations were in progress, Adolf Hoel, at that time director of what is now the Norwegian Polar Institute, was on a visit to Berlin. When his friend, Ernst Hermann failed to turn up and Hoel was unable to get any information as to his whereabouts, he contacted Hermann's wife who told him that her husband was in Hamburg preparing for an Antarctic expedition. 'I understood immediately that this expedition was heading for the the same place that Norway was planning to occupy,' Hoel wrote later. For once, Norway was quick off the mark and shortly afterwards, on 14 January 1939, King Haakon VII signed the following proclamation: 'that part of the continental coast which stretches from the Falkland Dependencies in the west (the limits of Coats Land) to the limits of the Australian Antarctic Dependency in the East (45° East longitude), together with all territory within this coastline and adjacent waters, are to be taken under Norwegian sovereignty.'

Lars Christensen was the first to 'discover' Queen Maud Land through the many expeditions he financed from 1927 until World War II. Here he is pictured on a rhinoceros hunt in Africa on his way to the Antarctic.

This proclamation was issued the day before the Germans sighted their first iceberg, and five days before the first German plane took off to begin its survey of the area. In the course of 17 days the Schwabenland dispatched seven flights across the ice-cap, surveying uncharted land. This included the Gessnertind mountain (named after the director of the Hansa aerial photography company) and extensive parts of the Wohlthat massif. Unfortunately most of this material disappeared after World War II, but the maps which were stored on board ship are still intact and show amongst other things where the darts with swastikas had been dropped.

That the Germans were not particularly popular in the Antarctic is obvious from Ernst Hermann's notes: 'Norwegian whalers regard us as pirates and thieves, down here with the sole purpose of invading territories, which in their view, have been granted them by God himself.' From the same jottings it seems clear that Adolf Hitler wasn't very popular either. 'As soon as we went ashore we were accosted by a native (penguin) whom we greeted with the Heil Hitler sign. He was not impressed.'

The 'Schwabenland' was received with military honours and greetings from Hitler on returning to Germany on 10 April 1939. Four months later, flouting the Norwegian claim, the Germans issued a decree establishing a German Antarctic Sector between 4°59' and 16°30' East longitude. After the war there was some speculation as to whether Adolf Hitler and Eva Braun had retreated to a new 'Berchtesgaden' (refuge) in Antarctica which, according to rumour, had been prepared by the expedition in 1939.

Soon after the second world war, a U.S Navy Antarctic expedition (Operation High Jump 1946-1947) flew over parts of Queen Maud Land. Since this expedition had military connotations, very little has been made public. Only the areas east of the twentieth meridian were photographed.

In 1950 a Norwegian, John Giæver led the first international expedition to the Antarctic. During two winters, (1950 and 1951), Norwegians, Swedes and Englishmen, working from the Norwegian base at Maudheim, conducted research in a variety of scientific disciplines. The area of operations was given the name Maudheimvidda (Maudheim plateau'), with Jutulstraumen ('The Stream of the Titans') its eastern boundary. Fenriskjeften and Norway's Highest Mountain were still a long distance away and when the expedition set off for home in 1952, only the Germans had yet seen Ulvetanna.

Members of the Norwegian Antarctic Expedition 1956-1960 (led by Sigurd Helle) were actually the second to see Ulvetanna. Throughout the Antarctic summer 1958-1959 the Wohlthat massif was charted, using both aerial photography and land surveying. Based on this material, Fenriskjefta ('The Wolf's Jaw') and Ulvetanna ('The Wolf's Fang') received their telling names. Had it been realised at the time that Jokulkyrkja was actually Norway's Highest Mountain, then perhaps it would have been given a name more in keeping with Roald Amundsen's and Lars

The Norwegian Antarctic Expedition passed north of Ulvetanna in January 1959. After the Germans' overflight in 1939, this was the second expedition to photograph it.

Sources: Reader's Digest, 'Antarctica'. John Giæver, 'Maudheim'. Roald Amundsen, 'Sydpolen'. Conversations with Sigurd Helle of the Norwegian Polar Institute and a historical summary by Hans Christian Erlandsen and Angela Amoroso.

Christensen's practice of commemorating the Norwegian royal family. With Haakon VII's plateau to the south and princes and princesses all down the coast, Mt. King Olav would have been so much more appropriate than Jokulkyrkja ('The Glacier Church', with its Ibsen-like overtones) for Norway's Highest Mountain in Queen Maud Land.

In 1993 a helicopter from the Norwegian Polar Institute landed on the top of Norway's Highest Mountain and fixed its height at 3148m, almost 700 m. higher than Galdhøpiggen (the highest summit in mainland Norway - 2469m). Although one cannot exactly call a helicopter landing a bona fide ascent, I was glad Fenriskjeften's pinnacles were too jagged to accommodate a helicopter, but anyway Ulvetanna had to submit to being photographed for the third time in history.

In my own very personal view, I choose to consider Queen Maud Land every bit as Norwegian as the country in which we spend our daily lives. This despite the fact that few countries have recognized Norway's Antarctic claims, and that future trends favour a single world nature reserve rather than fragmentation into sovereign areas. My conception of things is based on a purely egotistic love for this Norway in the South. Being Norwegian, we have a close affinity with mountains covered in snow.

Members of the Norwegian Antarctic Expedition 1956-60 digging a snow tractor out of a glacier crevasse.

The Dream of
Queen Maud Land

'You must remember that the highest isn't necessarily the best. Come over here young man and I'll show you mountains of which the world has never seen the like.' Sigurd Helle gripped my arm and made it quite clear that the search for Norway's Highest Mountain was over.

We were in the aerial photograph archives of the Norwegian Polar Institute. It was already half past eight in the evening and we had been at it for nearly five hours. Earlier in the day, I had been reading that everything over 6,000 feet in Norway had already been climbed. But what about Spitsbergen, Jan Mayen or Queen Maud Land? Did any of these places boast peaks of more than 6,000 feet? I had rung the Polar Institute and spoken with Sigurd Helle, the man who knows Queen Maud Land best. He led the Norwegian Antarctic Expedition in 1956-1960, and has probably spent more time continually in the Antarctic than anyone else alive or dead. That he had been retired for several years had not affected his working day in the least - far from it.

'Up north, there's only Jan Mayen with a single peak over 6,000 feet, in Queen Maud Land there are hundreds of them.' He answered as if this were something self-evident. The working day was over, but Helle had offered to stay

behind - if I was interested in maps and photographs. I was. My first question naturally was the name and altitude of Norway's Highest Mountain. However, this turned out to be something that had never bothered him. 'I don't know,' he admitted. 'It never occurred to us to think about it.' *Could it really be the case that Sigurd Helle, the polar veteran, did not even know the name or the correct altitude of the highest mountain in Queen Maud Land, and therefore the Kingdom of Norway? Were there still a few white blanks left upon the map?* I had the feeling that my quest had taken a completely new turning. I could feel the excitement building up in my solar plexus - while Helle brought out the charts maps he had.

Most of Queen Maud Land had been photographed from the air only once, and little or no field work had been carried out in the mountain massifs. In Sør-Rondane to the east, we discovered peaks of 12,000 feet, but this turned out to be wrong. The correct height was probably 2,000 ft less. Many of the old maps were totally misleading. In the end we settled for the Jøkulkyrkja massif where the Kyrkjeskipet ('The Nave') was marked off as the highest point, 3096m, and still it seemed as if there might be higher points further in on the plateau. In this region lay Norway's Highest Mountain, higher than Galdhøpiggen, without a single cairn on the summit. I was then busy route. Ulvetanna became my goal. I was setting my sights on the most difficult route on the most difficult mountain. The route represented an important goal in itself because it was so bound up with prestige.

Stein agreed with me. Ulvetanna was a goal of world class. But to climb the world's most difficult mountain we had to have the world's best mountaineers. Neither Stein nor I filled the bill. Undoubtedly, Stein was the one with the most experience. He had climbed Trango, in the Himalayas, but that was many years before. I was only a tyro and, as such, had to seek support from others.

For the moment, Queen Maud Land had to remain a Never-Never land. The 'Five of the Seven Summits'

organizing the Five of the Seven Summits expedition, but on the instant I made my decision: I would go to Queen Maud and and make the first ascent of Norway's Highest Mountain.

Some weeks later I was sitting with Stein P. Aasheim, the explorer and mountaineer, in his kitchen, and expounding my new plans. Odd Eliassen was also present. Stein thought it incredible that nobody had thought of it before. The ascent of Norway's Highest Mountain was one of the things that had never been done before - not just a new twist to stale deeds. What really intrigued them were all the aerial photographs of Fenriskjeften that Helle had pressed on me when I left the Institute. A wonderland with kilometre high pinnacles and rock walls rose straight up from an icefield of enormous proportions. Even among these wonders Ulvetanna was in a class of its own. The biggest fang in the whole of the Jaws of the Wolf, it sent shivers down your spine whatever comparisons you made. This was the perfect mountain queen; steep and treacherous on every side; isolated, unclimbed and virginal; beautiful, frigid and dangerous. There were three huge 1,000 metre walls, separated by sharp, impassable ridges. It was so steep and forbidding that - perish the thought - this mountain might simply not allow itself to be climbed in the course of the four weeks we reckoned to have at our disposal.

Intermingled with the longing to conquer, to try conclusions, to be the first, fear also loomed: fear of failure, fear of frostbite with lasting injury, and deep down, fear of death itself. I also had the fear of failing Ninja, Nick and Philip back home - waiting for Daddy: a father who went to the other end of the globe simply to satisfy his own urge to climb, conquer, be a real man, and win recognition. His motives were mixed, his arguments often specious; the search for unspoiled Nature, comradeship, sounded so much better than being first, scaling the heights and winning. I am quite frankly a competitive human being. The goal is just as important as the expedition was here and now. 'Five summits on five continents in five weeks' had never before been attempted. We would be the first to do it in our own particular way, and in the process, Ralph Høibakk and Arne Næss would be the first Norwegians to achieve the 'Seven Summits'. Round the world in five weeks would be a demanding tour, though not exactly a piece of pioneering. All our chosen mountains had been done before, back and front, by young and old, solo and in teams, by men and women- and now finally against the clock. The attraction lay not in the unknown, but in whether we would attain the goal we ourselves had defined.

Queen Maud Land would be different. No human being had ever before set foot there. The aerial photographs were old; taken from a considerable altitude thirty years ago. They showed few details, and would be of little help. We had butterflies in the stomach, simply thinking about planning and carrying out an expedition where none had been before. First Norway's Highest Mountain, then Ulvetanna. The dream of discovering the mountain world of Queen Maud Land was born.

Ivar Erik Tollefsen

13 - A Lucky Number!

For the thirteen of us who went to Queen Maud Land, this was a lucky number, but there was an enormous amount of work to do before we were ready to start. Stein and Odd, the first to see the pictures of Queen Maud Land, were an obvious choice from the start in the autumn of 1991. The three of us agreed that the best thing would be to get together a sizeable expedition comprising two teams of climbers, a skiing team and a base camp team with a cameraman and a communications expert. We were to go where no one had gone before and felt the responsibility of achieving as much as possible during the month we were to spend there.

In the autumn of 1992 I therefore asked the Polar Institute for permission to join their ship to Queen Maud Land the following season. I never received a proper reply, but after a long telephone conversation with Olav Orheim, the Institute's expedition leader, I realized that it was not going to be easy. The Polar Institute was financed by the State, and had no desire to let a small group of adventurers intrude on their subsidized existence. The expense of chartering our own ship was prohibitive; the only alternative seemed a long air journey by Twin Otter or DC3 from Punta Arenas in Chile: first south to Patriot Hills, and then along the coast via fuel depots established earlier on. This solution held few attractions, either on grounds of cost or constraints of time. A few years earlier, Ralph Hoibakk had had to kick his heels for weeks on end in Punta Arenas waiting for the weather to mend so that he could to fly to Mt. Vinson. In the end he returned to Norway having seen nothing but the airport. I did not relish the thought that this might be our fate as well. Awful to contemplate, on a large, heavily sponsored expedition like ours where we risked spending other people's money without even setting foot in the Antarctic.

Jan Erling Haugland at the Norwegian Polar Institute (unofficially) hinted that the Russians might be willing to take a private expedition on one of their ice breakers for a goodly sum of western currency. For many years the Russians had been running some form of commercial transport for other nations, and they responded to my enquiries promptly and professionally. As it turned out, they must have needed vast quantities of western currency - or else they had grasped what transport to the Antarctic was really worth. The price they quoted was not much less than other alternatives. At the beginning of May 1993 I nonetheless visited St. Petersburg and met Valery Lukin. He was head of RAE (Russian Antarctic Expeditions), and had considerable experience with expeditions in the Arctic and Antarctic. His institute had over 600 employees in St. Petersburg housed in a modern building in Bering Street. Lena, Lukin's secretary who met me at the airport, led me down endless corridors, finally ending up in Lukin's spacious corner office. Lena both spoke, and wrote, perfect English and was my guide and interpreter for the whole of my stay.

The Russians' written reply, received some weeks previously, had seemed professional and reassuring. On the other hand, when I saw photographs of the snow

tractors and helicopters which were to transport us from the coast to our base camp, I began to have second thoughts. The equipment was ancient and badly maintained. The helicopters looked as if they would crash at any moment, and as for the snow tractors, they did not seem built to run at all. Strange, I thought, that for decades the world has stood in awe of Russian military might. From what I had seen of Russian technology up to now, everything was ancient, unwieldy and badly in need of repair. The same went for the office building we were sitting in; grimy and well worn, although it had been built only ten years ago. My only consolation was that the Russians had five bases in the Antarctic and they themselves put their trust in this equipment. Presumably they were as fond of their lives as we are of ours. It took me the best part of a month to sign an agreement with the Russians, which included transport by sea from Cape Town to the Russian Novo base, and the use of helicopter and tractor to our Base Camp inland.

With the transport in the bag, there remained only the little matter of men and money. Financing an expedition is always a long and complicated task, and this one coinciding as it did with the Lillehammer Winter Olympics hardly made things easier. Without a solid core of satisfied sponsors from the 'Five of the Seven Summits' expedition, we would never have managed in the three months we had at our disposal.

It was at this stage that I met the Norwegian painter, Vebjørn Sand, who was keen to accompany us to Queen Maud Land. Vebjørn was very taken with the thought of being the first artist in a region where no human beings had ever been before. It was almost like being presented with your very own country, which you alone would be privileged to interpret to the outside world. The aerial photos portrayed a land of wild and rugged scenery, quite different from anything we had seen before. Fenriskjeften and Ulvetanna were mystic names conjuring up visions of supernatural mountains and forces beyond our ken. In Vebjørns eyes I could see a boy's dream of conquering new lands – the first to ascend Norway's Highest Mountain! Vebjørn intended climbing right to the top, not just sitting around Base Camp with palette, brush and easel. We decided on a trip to Svalbard to introduce him to the art of climbing in the polar regions. Vebjørn took it all very seriously. All autumn long he was out running, cycling or fell-walking with a rucksack filled with rocks. He spent days in the low temperature laboratory of the Ministry of Defence, learning how to paint in thirty degrees of frost. The military authorities

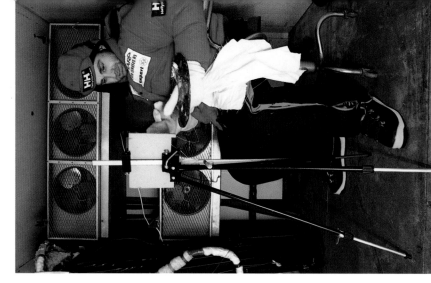

Vebjørn Sand took his preparations seriously, spending several hours in the low temperature laboratory at the Norwegian Ministry of Defence practising painting in thirty degrees of frost.

provided him with a personal heater for his body and warm leads for his fingers and toes. Thus equipped, he could sit for hours on end, without feeling the cold too much. I had great faith in Vebjørn's paintings as illustrations for the book. I looked forward to seeing what he would make of the scenery in our Norway in the south. The combination of paintings and photographs would be most exciting.

Early that autumn I had a telephone call from Stein. He had had an offer from the Norwegian Broadcasting Corporation (NRK) to present a television adventure

---

The skiing party

ODD ELIASSEN (50)
All round expedition experience from many years in the game. First ascent of Trollveggen in 1965. Norwegian Everest expedition 1985, Five of the Seven Summits expedition in 1992, to name but a few. Prefers skiing to climbing. Skiing party.

JO TOFTDAHL (35)
Accompanied Odd and Stein twice across Greenland. Tough and tireless. Skiing party.

BÅRD STOKKAN (34)
Ivar's right hand man throughout the whole of the planning phase. No great climber, nonetheless an experienced expedition man from the Greenland and Five of the Seven Summits expeditions. Skiing party.

VEBJØRN SAND (28)
One of Norway's best known younger painters and controversial debater. Surprisingly fit, for an artist. Everybody liked Vebjørn and went out of their way to give him the best conditions in which to work. Base Camp.

ERIK S. NIELSEN (34)
Engineer and childhood friend of Ivar and Bård. Joined us as communications expert and ended up as jack of all trades. Skier and climbing partner. Base camp.

CARL EMIL PETERSEN (69)
Sailed with the Rundø round Svalbard and along the coast of East Greenland. First solo crossing of Greenland at the age of 58. Author of five travel books. Took part in the last lap of the Nordre-expedition to the South Pole in 1990. A great support and a wonderful companion. Base Camp.

JAN PALMERS (30)
Swedish, with Norwegian wife. Television cameraman and the expedition's technological whizz-kid. We had to hide our private Walkmen and other electronic accessories from Jan to save then from being cannibalised for his inventions. Base camp.

The Alpine Party

JAN ÅGE GUNDERSEN (32)
All round and active climber and skier. On the Five of the Seven Summits attempt on Anconcagua. Alpine team.

ROBERT CASPERSEN (22)
Norwegian indoor climbing champion at the age of twenty. No previous expedition experience, but impressed everyone with his thorough, all-round ability. Alpine team.

Boris Yeltsin put a spoke in the wheel for the expedition.

series at prime time on Saturday evenings, and reluctantly chose to stay at home. Aslak Aastorp and Bjørn Myrer Lund were two other experienced climbers, who also had to withdraw in the course of the autumn. Both were expecting to become fathers about the time we would be returning from the Antarctic.

Nonetheless, we had no difficulty collecting two teams of elite mountaineers. Everyone I contacted agreed that this was the most exciting Norwegian expedition for many years. They were more than ready for the first ascent of Norway's Highest Mountain. American-born Thomas Cosgriff leaped at the chance, threatening to resign from his job if his employers refused to give him leave. Bård put himself at the head of the queue when there was talk of redundancy where he worked. Robert broke off his studies in France, Jan Åge was a student with plenty of spare time, and Sjur would much rather scale mountains than work at his carpenter's job in Tromsø in the winter. 'You've just made me Tromsø's happiest man,' was Sjur's reply when I rang to ask him if he wanted to come. Carl Emil was our beloved father figure, Trond had long been waiting for a trip to Antarctica and Jo's name had been down on our list since 1991 when Odd and Stein blurted out our plans. By a quirk of fate the main team now consisted of climbers of whom I had only slight knowledge. Sjur, Trond and Thomas had all known each other for donkey's years. It was I who was the outsider. This turned out to pose a problem.

Boris Yeltsin was the next to put a spoke in our wheel. Riots during the autumn of 1993 paralysed the whole Russian administration, with the result that the Polar Institute in St. Petersburg had to wait for their money. The Russian ice breaker Akademik Fedorov, which should have left St. Petersburg in the middle of October, was still there at the beginning of November. Without money it was impossible to get the crew to sign on for the voyage. Our plan had been to sail with the ice breaker on her second journey from Cape Town to the Antarctic, but with over a month's delay it would be the end of February, and almost winter, before we reached the mountains of Queen Maud Land. The only course that remained was to join the ice breaker on her first voyage, which promised to be some time in the middle of December.

Three weeks' less time for planning and packing turned our orderly chaos into unrelieved panic. We accepted bitterly that many important details would have to be ignored, but now it was a matter of getting the vital things done. Christmas, which we had hoped to spend in Norway with our wives and children before leaving for two months, was now out of the question. Yeltsin became a dirty word.

The wall team

THOMAS COSGRIFF (36)
An American from Boulder, Colorado. Has lived and worked in Norway since 1989. Without doubt our strongest big wall climber. Repeated the Arch Wall (Trollveggen) in 1992 with Aslak Aastorp. In the 'eighties one of America's most active aid climbers, having scaled some of the world's most difficult rock-faces. Wall team.

SJUR NESHEIM (42)
Hardbitten type from Northern Norway. More winter experience than anyone else. Climbed Trollveggen in the winter of 1982. Climbing is a vital part of Sjur's life. Wall team.

TROND HILDE (32)
The expedition's strongest all-rounder. Equally good on skis, steep ice and extreme routes. Experience from climbing expedition to Peru in 1988. Wall team.

IVAR ERIK TOLLEFSEN (33)
The expedition's initiator and leader. Wall team.

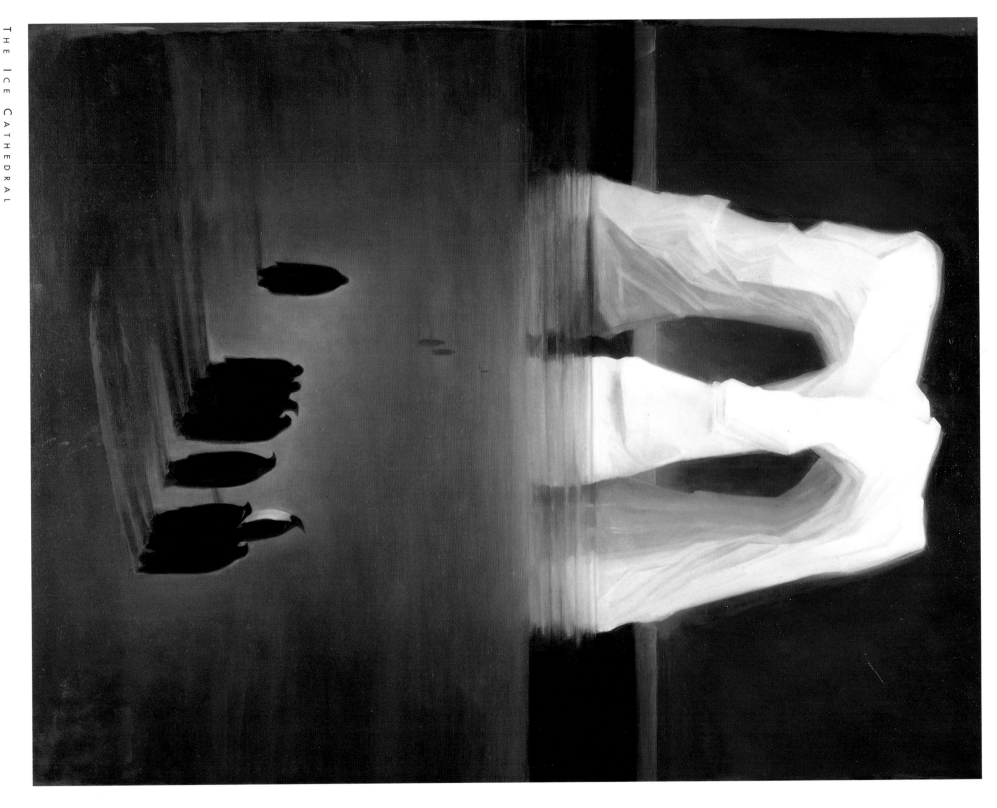

A Russian Christmas

With every day that passed without the Akademik Fedorov leaving St. Petersburg, our hopes of spending Christmas in Norway rose. Our air tickets were changed from day to day, almost driving the Lufthansa people insane. When the ice breaker finally sailed from St. Petersburg on 23 November, it was still not clear whether she would leave Cape Town before or after Christmas Eve. It was finally on 21 December that the message came through to us in Norway; the Akademik Fedorov was to leave Cape Town at precisely two p.m. on Christmas Eve. That very same evening we fetched the Christmas tree in and decorated the house. The next day we celebrated Christmas Eve in advance, with traditional Norwegian fare and presents under the tree. Bård came in from the garage where he had been packing and joined us for 'Christmas' dinner. When the children at last fell asleep in my bed I felt at peace with myself. Our 'Christmas' was at least as good as other Christmases. The children had been just as excited and the pile of presents amazed me as before me. The aquavit warmed the cockles of my heart. I felt I could set out on my travels with a good conscience. All autumn I had been thinking I ought to spend Christmas at home for the sake of the children. Now I realized it really meant as much to me too. Trond was equally happy and contented when he arrived that same night to continue packing, after a successful Christmas celebration at home.

Fornebu airport on the day before Christmas Eve is the busiest day of the whole year. We added to the chaos in the departure lounge, with a horde of journalists, photographers, TV-wallahs, grannies, wives, offspring and well wishers in our wake, besides two tons of climbing equipment which had to be labelled and handed in like ordinary luggage.

'Forty eight pieces of luggage all told.' From the Five of the Seven Summits expedition Bård had learned the importance of an overview.

'Have you included Jan's tripod?'

'No, I thought it was hand luggage.'

'How many labels did they give us, and how many have we got left?'

'We had fifty and we've used them all up.' Bård was suddenly worried. Was it fifty or only forty nine? He wanted to count them all over again, but with half the baggage already checked in, it was too late.

We were all glad to relax on the plane, get away from packing, the insistent ringing of the phone and all the fuss. I stole a look at the gang, thinking how odd they all looked in brand-new fleece jackets covered in sponsor logos. Like some sports team from the boondocks on their first trip to the Big City. There was no turning back now - adventure awaited us. Up to now, Bård and I had been more or less on our own. Now we were thirteen excited boys on the way to the adventure of our lives. I fell asleep as we taxied onto the runway, dreaming I'd missed the local ferry-boat. Was this an omen that we were to miss the last boat out from the Antarctic before winter set in? Many an expedition before us had been forced to overwinter against its will.

The heat battered us when we disembarked at Cape Town. With German precision, Lufthansa landed exactly on time. Akademik Fedorov had already loaded all her cargo, and was

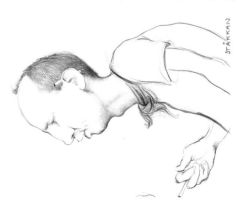

waiting only for us. Her captain had said two o'clock, and not a second later. One and a half hours for passport control, customs and transport out to the ship was cutting it very fine. Happily, Bård's mother, Jorun, as on previous expeditions, had eased our path. Jens Otterbech, the Norfwegian Ambassador, was waiting for us at the air terminal, and had us quickly through passport control. Customs control was waived altogether, allowing us a short time in Cape Town for last minute shopping: a diary, new biros, and bathing trunks for the first few days on board.

Carl Emil, Vebjørn, Robert and Sjur were already waiting for us on the quayside, sunburned and almost bouncing up and down with excitement. They had already been here a week and stowed away provisions needed for two months' absence from civilization. Meat, bread, fresh vegetables and fruit, Coca-Cola, beer, benzine for the primus stoves, champagne for New Year's Eve and crate after crate of the more or less (mostly less) necessary items Bård had had on his list. All our 50 (or was it 49?) pieces of luggage were hoisted on board while we

From Christmas slush in Norway to summer sunshine in South Africa. With German precision we landed exactly on time, but with a ton of luggage and 90 minutes before the ship sailed, it was a mad rush through the streets of Cape Town.

Many of Mikkel's friends at nursery school wondered why his daddy had to go all the way to Africa to climb a tooth.

More haste, less speed. In the final rush before our departure, packing got the upper hand, and our planned 1,500 kg soon mushroomed to 2,000. Luckily we had a long journey before us, and everything sorted itself out by the time we reached Novo.

stood thanking the Ambassador and the rest of the Otterbech family before walking up the gangway. We all had butterflies in our stomachs. Many previous expeditions had sailed from Cape Town en route for Antarctic adventure, never to return. The waters between Cape Town and Queen Maud Land are the most treacherous in the world. Those latitudes have been named after the cacophony of the wind. The Roaring Forties, the Screaming Fifties and the Howling Sixties are well known terms among seamen the world over. Most of the party already had seasick plasters behind their ears - it was to be prepared. My unease however, did not concern the crossing. The Russians had done the voyage many times without mishap. The North Wall of Ulvetanna was another magtter altogether. None of us could know what the next few weeks were to bring of toil, fear and cold. I was both looking forward to it and dreading it.

The Akademik Fedorov did not sail before half past five. Gradually it dawned on us that time was a fluid concept to our new-found Russian friends. Lena, Lukin's secretary, whom I had already met in St. Petersburg, had been spending the last week in Cape Town together with Vebjørn and the others. She acted as our interpreter, and liaison with the Russians throughout the whole trip. When we were in the climbing region, she would be standing by at the Novo base in case we needed radio-contact. Lena told us she had had quite a shock when she met Carl Emil, Robert, Sjur and Vebjørn at Frankfurt airport. She was convinced that Robert was a girl and foresaw considerable problems on board with a special cabin in an already crowded boat. Great was her relief when Robert opened his mouth, revealing that he was definitely male in spite of his mop of red hair. Lena's almost perfect command of English had given her a special position as an interpreter at the Russian polar institute. She was involved in nearly all international projects, travelling extensively abroad, even before the Soviet Union opened its borders. Lena wore her dyed hair scraped back into a rat's-tail and sported thick layers of lipstick, scarlet nails and an American tote bag. None of the gang was interested in Lena at first, but as time passed, and the number of girls remained constant, she won us over with her charm. In fact, she was the cause of a regular cock-fight between two members of the expedition, who shall be nameless.

The Akademik Fedorov was a big and splendid ship, built in Finland in the 'eighties and surprisingly well appointed. We had four-man cabins, with shower, lavatory and writing desk. Next door we had South Africans and Germans. *The Akademik Fedorov's* first port of call in the Antarctic turned out to be the South African base, SANAE. After about a week for discharging cargo, we would continue on to our destination; the ice shelf off the Russian Novo-base. The Germans were to sail further with the ship on her long journey round the Antarctic.

Bård and I had planned some Norwegian Christmas festivities, and after the other passengers left the saloon, we had it at our disposal for a private party. We laid the table, folding napkins into boat shapes. We listened soberly as Vebjørn read us the Christmas gospel, whilst our plastic tree vibrated to the movements of the ship. Cured meats, home-made crispbread and the indispensable aquavit tasted almost as good as our Christmas dinner at home two days earlier. Santa Claus had gifts for one and all. In the course of the evening we rigged up a satellite dish and everyone was were able to ring home to their families and wish them a Merry Christmas. Many months of hectic preparations were over. My maxim of celebrating all my successes in advance (otherwise you'll never celebrate anything) was promptly followed to the letter. Next day even Odd and Carl Emil stayed in bed until late.

We enjoyed fine weather for the whole of the crossing, and sighted our first icebergs just after passing Bouvetoya. From their appearance they were several years old. Almost pale green in colour with their surface snow and sharp edges long since melted and washed away. The air grew colder day by day. The captain's daily bulletins announced water and air temperatures around zero. Wind speeds of 15-20 metres a second sounded a lot, but it hardly affected the ship at all, and the sea was fairly calm. While the Akademik Fedorov forged ahead at 16-17

Ho, ho, ho. Are there any good children here?

It doesn't matter if you don't know all the words. I've got it on tape!

Under the influence of Russian vodka, Sjur went through a change of personality. His voice sank several octaves, and his North Norwegian dialect was replaced with English 'It's gonna be hard, man.'

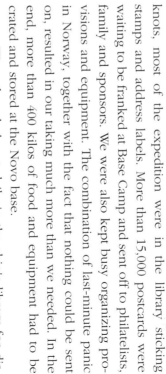

This is better than being Santa Claus in a kindergarten!

Bård was responsible for Norwegian-Russian relations at grassroots level and had an impressive assortment of trading goods. A T-shirt for a bottle of vodka, two Olympics badges or a postmark for a glass of coffee etc.

knots, most of the expedition were in the library sticking stamps and address labels. More than 15,000 postcards were waiting to be franked at Base Camp and sent off to philatelists, family and sponsors. We were also kept busy organizing provisions and equipment. The combination of last-minute panic in Norway, together with the fact that nothing could be sent on, resulted in our taking much more than we needed. In the end, more than 400 kilos of food and equipment had to be crated and stored at the Novo base.

We gathered almost daily in the ship's library for discussions. We could have done without most of them as many of the issues we argued over, solved themselves automatically when the expedition got under way. This also applied to the Great Pooh Problem. It was official policy that all human

excrement had to be removed from Antarctica. This was a general condition we had when we planned the expedition. However, it is one thing to decide such things at home, but not quite the same when you have to put it into practice. Most of us now voted for taking our garbage out with us on our return, but leaving our excrement behind. I had to agree that this was the easiest solution, but it irritated me to see how easily rules could be broken. Thomas reckoned it would be impossible to climb Ulvetanna hampered by these kind of restrictions. It was my opinion that the treaty countries responsible for the regulations, literally didn't give a damn whether we climbed Ulvetanna or not. The whole point was that we were supposed to adapt our activities to the regulations and not the other way about. By being the first, we had the opportunity to set the standards, and trust that those who came after us abided by them. In practice, it was nonetheless Thomas and others who turned out to be right. Neither I nor anyone else managed to remove all human excrement. Even if 'invisible spoor' is a time-honoured concept among Norwegian mountaineers, it is not unknown for someone to plant a flag or leave a 'mind-where-you-tread' on the summit. We agreed to do without this kind of thing, and simply build cairns in the interests of a cleaner environment.

The composition of our teams and the the expedition's aims were worked out before we

left. Morning meetings soon revealed that what had seemed sensible at home was not going to work in the field. Thomas insisted on climbing the north wall with only two, at most three, men. He feared it might be too dangerous having four men in two different hanging tents. Nor was he sure whether he wanted me in the team either, since I had absolutely no experience of big wall climbing. Thomas's objection was possibly justified, but he had evidently forgotten that it was he who was with me and not the other way about. My lack of big wall experience was common knowledge from the outset, but I still had to suppress an urge to heave Thomas over board. I was aghast that one of our members should want to exclude me from a project I had been working on for so long. Besides, in climbing a big wall in the Antarctic, it is not *only* experience that counts, but stamina, determination, and the ability to tolerate extreme cold. When Thomas was at his most flattering I was the ideal big wall climber who had all these qualities, but now it seemed that the only man he trusted was Sjur. Sjur probably agreed with him, but kept a low profile, while Trond insisted that this was agreed as a four man job, and that was that. It would all sort itself out when we got there, was my secret hope.

Robert and Jan Age were our alpine team. Instead of attempting a big wall project, they would do easier routes on a number of mountains in alpine style, using minimum equipment and without any bivouacs on the way. The aerial photographs indicated that the north-west wall of Ulvetanna could probably be accomplished by the alpine team in the course of a day or so. Thomas objected that it didn't seem fair that the alpine team should have the honour of being first to the top when the wall team would invest so much time and energy on the north wall. He thought the alpine team should keep off Ulvetanna altogether. Once more it turned out that we'd been seeing problems where no problems existed. In point of fact, the camera lied. The north-west wall proved to be a demanding wall climb with many nights spent in hanging bivouacs; with frostbite and difficult climbing.

In accordance with my plan, the expedition was to make a joint attempt on Jøkulkyrkja, Norway's Highest Mountain. Odd was sceptical. First he expressed doubts that the skiing team would be able to make it round the Wohlthat massif in

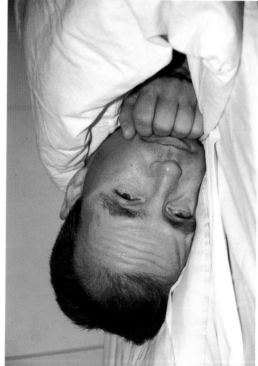

Do I have to get up now?

time, next wondered whether all of us were in physical condition to reach the top! For the umpteenth time since I met Odd three years ago, I was fed up with the way he always concentrated on the negative. When it was just the two of us it was allright. Then Odd was if possible even more of an optimist than I am, but with the gang he consistently played the role of Cassandra. He clearly felt that with three amateurs in our midst, it was important to emphasize the dangers, while I for my part was afraid that insecurity might be more dangerous than respect.

The next day Robert went missing. I searched the hold, his cabin, the upper deck, but he had vanished. Probably nothing serious, but over the past few days a couple of homosexuals in the Russian crew had been displaying an unseemly interest. One of them was big and powerfully built, and Robert had voiced the fear of one day being dragged into a Russian cabin without warning. In the end I found him in the library where he was sitting as a model for Vebjørn's first portrait. Vebjørn not only took his turn licking stamps and drawing caricatures for the book. He had also started painting portraits and drawing caricatures for the book. He was definitely not lazy, and was much less Bohemian than we had expected.

Four meals a day sounds like a Caribbean cruise, but Russian cooking does not exactly conjure up visions of palm trees and sun-drenched beaches. Even a courteous lad like Jo, from Oslo's west end, was heard to remark that every meal tasted bloody Russian. Next day Jo's place was empty. The Akademik's rolling excused him from further meals. Nor did Bård wish to ruin his refined palate, developed through years of patronising Oslo's restaurants. He often absented himself from breakfast and lunch. Odd, on the other hand, boasted uninhibitedly about every single meal (this was before they started serving liver) and always asked for a second helping. The two girls in the galley fell hopelessly in love with him, and several evenings we were treated to the sight of two vodka-happy wenches searching for Odd's cabin, without finding our gourmandising charmer. Odd was usually hidden behind the curtain or under Erik's bed.

The Russians were used to expeditions like ours having their own special postal cancellation stamps and commemorative covers. Russian collectors' zeal easily equalled the hysterical Norwegian interest in Olympic badges *before* Lillehammer. When word got about that we had an official post office franking stamp which could only be used at our base camp between certain dates, their enthusiasm knew no bounds. Bård, who had taken upon himself the role of liaison officer for Russo-Norwegian affairs at grass roots level, promptly added ready-stamped postcards to his assortment of wares. A T-shirt for a bottle of vodka, two badges or a postmark for a coffee glass, and so on. Bård had not invested much time in training before leaving Norway. Now with Bård himself, Sjur and Robert celebrating into the small hours with the Russian crew. Odd and Jo became worried about Bård's physical condition as a member of the skiing team. Moreover, I was becoming fed up with Sjur waking me up in the middle of the night to borrow a loudspeaker for his walkman - or having long and serious discussions on scaling big walls. Russian vodka had done things to him. His broad Tromsø dialect was replaced by broken English, his voice sank several octaves and his face assumed a lugubrious expression. Such was the transformation I was convinced for a time that we had fourteen and not thirteen members in our expedition.

Vebjørn and Jan Åge indulged in long literary discussions that circled round Jung and Freud. Their scale of quality of life was who had read the most erudite literature. Once, when I tried to join in, Vebjørn soon shut me up when I was unable to name a single journalist on Aftenposten's arts staff. The remaining members of the expedition were the subject of a detailed psycho-analysis and brutal classification such as schizoids, psychopaths and other more or less serious deviants. Vebjørn would always, for example, start off haranguing me by saying something like: 'Ivar, I have seldom come across such a gifted person as you. It is therefore, quite beyond my comprehension that you appear to have the wits of a babe in arms when it comes to an intelligent appreciation of Norwegian intellectual life.'

Even with modern radar systems, icebergs are still a threat to shipping. We came across this one way up north. After drifting for many years, there was little left of dazzling white snow and crystal blue ice.

Princess Astrid Coast

Large parts of Antarctica are lined with ice shelves up to 30-50 metres high. The perpendicular ice front is formed when inland ice is forced out into the sea, calving in huge flat slabs, the so called tabular icebergs. One of the biggest and best known appeared in 1979 when Trolltunga broke off from the ice shelf off the coast of Queen Maud Land. This massive formation was as big as several English counties, and contained enough fresh water to supply the whole of Los Angeles for the next 1,000 years. Given such dimensions, it is small wonder that several expeditions have been landed on what they imagined to be the ice shelf, to discover that they were surrounded entirely by water.

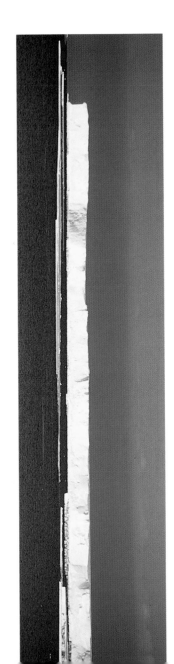

When the ice cap is forced out into the ocean, huge icebergs calve off to drift slowly north. To us, approaching by sea, it was as though the whole continent came floating towards us, welcoming us to a frigid world of snow and ice. In the course of New Year's Eve the pack ice tightened, and the captain did not expect to make the coast until the next morning. The New Year celebrations were nothing like as boisterous as those at Christmas, and early next morning Carl Emil and Odd went round waking everybody up, announcing that the ice front had been sighted in the distance. They both think that it is a great event each time they can wake anybody, and on that morning, therefore, they enjoyed one of their proudest moments. They took the view that if they were awake, then so should everybody else be. I leaped out of my lower bunk, and pulled on my down jacket. The top bunk was already vacated. Either Bård had got up before me or else he had never been to bed.

When came up on deck, the pack ice was tight on both sides of the ship. The Akademik was doing a maximum of 6-7 knots as she forced a passage through tons of snow and ice. We hung over the rails and watched in awe every time we rammed a huge floe, thrusting it forward before it broke in two, one of the halves rearing skywards while the sea water came cascading in torrents. In the distance, the ice front dominated the whole horizon, and just offshore, the South African vessel lay at anchor. The first stage was over. The rest of the week we would spend discharging materials and provisions for the new South African base. The weather was overcast, and with all the ice in the water, the horizon seemed to dissolve into a haze of grey and white. The previous day had been more picturesque with a deep blue sea and majestic icebergs. One rarely gets good pictures without proper light and contrast, so I left my camera in peace. Even with Kodak as one of our sponsors, we bit deep into our stock of film. Everyone took the same photographs of the same icebergs and the same sunset, with the result that we ended up with more than 1,000 iceberg pictures.

We could not anchor next to the South African ship, so the helicopter took off to find us a better berth in the vicinity. At first we considered this helicopter a museum piece from World War II, and various playful remarks were made as to which of us would dare to go on the first flight. The fact that it actually *flew* raised our hopes. Later that evening we sailed east, anchoring in a splendid bay with solid bay ice. The Russians were able to put cargo out on the ice here, while the helicopter shuttled between our ship and the South African base. It was a relief to be able to go ashore and get on our skis. To our delight the place was alive with seals and penguins. If we had stayed at the barrier we would probably have missed all this wildlife. Seals and penguins like best to be within reach of open water so that they can find their food. To prevent the crew from going penguin hunting, the Russian captain decided to hoist us ashore, rather than let down the gangway. Next morning, therefore, we were hoisted over the side, the sun shining out of a cloudless sky. As if by command, a small flock of Antarctica's diminutive natives came waddling along to greet us. Adélie penguins are even more inquisitive than the larger emperor penguins, and inspected everybody who came and went from the ship. It felt strange to approach such large wild animals without their showing any sign of fear. Many of the seals were so tame that we were able to tickle their bellies with our ski sticks, and then they merely rolled over on their sides, emitting a red gold stream of urine. One of them was snoring so fiercely that I was unable to wake him to take a picture. It was only when I tried to sit on him to eat my lunch, that he deigned to roll over on his side, giving me a reproachful look and promptly going to sleep again.

After having been cooped up for ten days on board ship, our activity on shore knew no bounds. Most of the group went on long skiing trips. Some climbed up the almost perpendicular ice front, using crampons and ice axes. The Russian captain warned us against the belt between the bay ice and the ice front. It was in constant movement, with the attendant risk of falling

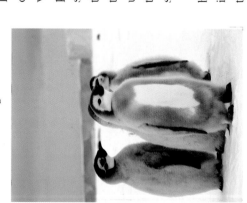

With their human appearance and inquisitive nature, penguins are charming creatures. Even if they can stand extreme cold, it often seems as if the chicks freeze in their down covering.

Even although ice often breaks off in huge slabs, it does not take long before wind and waves break them up into smaller pieces. The flat top indicates that this was probably a piece of the floating ice shelf off Queen Maud Land. Even although the size doesn't seem all that impressive, only 10% of it is visible. The rest is under water.

into a snow-covered lead. Nevertheless, it was here we spent most of our time. The climbers had to cross this belt to reach the foot of the ice front, and there we discovered cave. Odd had a nasty fright when he put one leg through the bay ice on his way into the cave, but that did not deter him from crawling further in. Once inside the cave, turning and looking back was like a religious experience. Here the ice had a strong, clear, blue white colour, with the fjord ice and the deep blue sea in stunning contrast in the distance. The entrance to the cave shimmered in a rosy-red light, reminiscent of the murals in old churches, where angels appear through a shining gap in the heavens. It was worth taking a risk for an experience like this, and we all crept in and out of the cave several times.

IT'S A HARD LIFE FOR PAPA PENGUIN

There are about 40 million penguins in Antarctica, where the emperor penguin, with its 40 kg and 120 cm (approximately, 47 inches) in height, is the largest. Penguins live mostly along the coast, but in April and May the females travel up to 100 km inland to lay their eggs. When the egg is laid, the male places it on his feet, covering it with a fold of skin, while the female makes her way back to the coast to fatten up. With winter temperatures of 50-60 degrees below zero, the male penguin has a hard 50 days and nights without food before the egg is hatched. By the time the female returns, he has lost almost half of his body-weight, and has scarcely any strength left to crawl out to the open water.

Adélie penguins are smaller than the colourful emperor penguins and much more inquisitive. Even before we went ashore a welcoming committee stood waiting for us on the ice.

After many days of inactivity on board, it was splendid having something to do again. The perpendicular ice front was ideal for climbing practice.

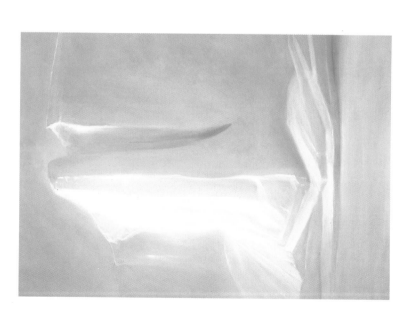

THE ICE SHELF

In the border zone between bay ice and ice shelf, we found a wonderful ice cave. Even with the constant danger from ice in motion, the experience was well worth the risk.

On the evening of 7 January our stay in the idyllic bay was coming to an end. The captain intended making for the ice front outside the Novo base next morning, and the crew were busy assembling a helicopter, which had hitherto been hidden in the hangar. Lena and I spent most of the evening with the Russian Chief of Expeditions and his chief pilot. Our flight path and landing places needed meticulous planning. Satellite pictures indicated that it would be difficult to find our way inland by tractor. The Russians therefore preferred to fly us directly in by helicopter. Lena was to stay behind, as a result of which the language barrier would prohibit explanations and changes of course along the way.

The pilots were apprehensive of the altitude, the length of the flight and, not least, the weight of our impedimenta. The helicopter was not designed to fly above 4,500 ft. Our base camp at the foot of the north wall of Ulvetanna happened to be 5,250 ft up. To give them a margin of safety from surrounding peaks they would have to fly at 7,500 ft. The heat of the sun

Alone but not lonely. Both Emperor and Adélie penguins are distinctly gregarious and hunt and breed in flocks. They have no natural enemies on land, and out to sea, they have in general only the leopard seal to fear.

on the rocks could result in violent fluctuations of temperature of between 40 and 50 degrees C., which entailed heavy turbulence and difficult flying conditions. To tell the truth, the Russians were in the same position as us; they were to fly over unknown territory without much hope of help if anything went wrong. They were plainly agitated despite the fact that their commander was an experienced, much decorated military pilot who, amongst other things, had once landed on the summit of Mt. Elbruz (5,645m above sea level; Europe's highest mountain). Admittedly that was in a modern helicopter, but still it was comforting to know that we were in safe hands and that our Russian friends were taking their task seriously.

All in all we were to make three flights. The first would be to the foot of Ulvetanna where we were to set up our Base Camp. Then eight of our party were to be flown to an advanced starting point for the ascent of Jokulkyrkja, and finally the remaining five to the same point. The first trip was the most exciting; we were to get our first glimpse of Ulvetanna, and everyone wanted to be first. The trouble was that the helicopter could only take three passengers. I, as leader, was the obvious first choice, then cameraman Jan. But who should be third man? Odd, who was one of the skiing party, argued that this would be his only chance of seeing Ulvetanna and Fenriskjeften close to. The same went for Bård and Jo, but then as Odd put it: 'I am just longing to see those mountains.' Alas, for Odd, it was more important to have either Thomas or Sjur along to reconnoitre the wall team's route.

'I think I should go.' Thomas was convinced he was the most qualified. Sjur disagreed.

'I can't see why it has to be you,' he complained in his thick Tromsø dialect.

'Because I'm better qualified than you to pick out the correct route on a wall like Ulvetanna,' Thomas was not one to mince words.

'I reckon Sjur has more experience in this type of climbing,' broke in Trond before Sjur had time to answer.

'We'll draw lots,' I said, even although I had more faith in Thomas. Sjur won, and Thomas would have to wait a whole week before seeing the wall at close quarters.

The Russians did not propose giving helicopter No. 2 a test flight, and interest in flight DML 01 lessened considerably when it turned out to be the first trial of the Russians' method of assembly with shoddy rotor bolts. The expedition now entered its final hectic phase, while the Akademik forced its way eastwards through heavy pack ice. Nobody got much sleep that night. I was wide awake and feverish with excitement. The Dream of Queen Maud Land was about to come true.

After a week in the idyllic bay, we set out eastwards for the Novo barrier.

When the Russians put together their reserve helicopter we thought we were watching an old movie. Colours, crew, costumes seemed to come straight out of the 'fifties. We thought the helicopter must be that old too. With rotor bolts just hammered in, it was ready for take off to Ulvetanna Base Camp. Strangely, all argument as to who was to be on the first flight had petered out.

The First Ascent of the Highest Mountain in Norway

BACK!! The Russian helicopter pilot was waving his arms about, signalling Jan, Sjur and me to crawl to the rear of the helicopter. At this precise moment the motor was at maximum lift and maximum speed, but the helicopter slid over the ice with its tail in the air, its nose to the ground, and refused to lift a centimetre. We scrambled into the tail as fast as we could. Four of the Russian crew did likewise. The helicopter had a crew of five, two pilots, a navigator, a radio operator and a man to pull up the steps and throw smoke flare to establish wind direction on landing. The Chief of Expeditions was also on board to survey the territory for crevasses in the glaciers for future use of tractors. The commander yelled in my ear, waving a paper showing how our starting weight was calculated down to the last kilogram. Now it began to dawn on me why we could not become airborne. I could not really credit that his margins were that small, and had cheated by a couple of hundred kilos. Had I not done so, none of us would have flown in the helicopter at all. I was about to confess my sins when a sudden cheer went up, and looking out of the window I could see that we were almost a metre off the ground. Thank God! Slowly, slowly we continued to rise, until we levelled out at an altitude of some hundred metres en route for Ulvetanna. Happily, we were to fly quite a distance before it would become necessary to gain height. By that time I hoped we should have used so much fuel that we would be able to fly at a greater altitude.

Half an hour later the captain beckoned me into the cockpit. One of the pilots handed me his binoculars, pointing straight ahead. Because he wore glasses, it was some time before I could focus properly, but suddenly I saw a distant but familiar profile on the horizon. *Could this really be Ulvetanna more than 200 km away?* I could scarcely credit it, but the bearing was correct, and the profile was exactly as I had seen it in the old photographs at the Polar Institute. As we approached, all doubt vanished and soon I could see the summit pillar with the naked eye. Both pilots dug out their antique Russian cameras and started taking photographs. Jan was glued to the cockpit, his camera rolling furiously. Ulvetanna made a deep impression on all of us.

Ulvetanna was so big that even with only ten minutes flying time left, it still filled the horizon, but with Arnesteinen ahead and to the right, it dawned on me that there was still some distance to go. Level with the north summit of Fenristunga, the helicopter suddenly started circling, simultaneously losing height. It looked as though we were about to land, but this did not agree with my map. I tried to enter the cockpit but was unceremoniously shoved out. The crew were clearly worried about landing a heavily laden helicopter in a rarefied atmosphere with no observation for wind speed or direction. With the door open, there was an appalling cacophony of wind and noise. Our 'doorman' struck several matches before he managed to light the smoke flare, dropping it from a considerable height. Warily, we circled lower and

Jøkulkyrkja from the north west with the Cathedral opposite. The highest point lies approximately in the centre of the picture.

The helicopter, weighed down with too much baggage, kept sliding across the ice, refusing to become airborne. On our way we collided with oil barrels and other 'sundries' that were in the way.

lower round the smoke, which was rising straight up. The air was dead calm. The pilots kept the helicopter hovering an inch or two above ground while the 'doorman' jumped out to check that the surface was level and free of crevasses. Through the open door we saw him give the thumbs up sign. Our pilot slowly reduced the rotor speed until all three wheels sank deep into the snow. Even after giving the helicopter a test shake to make sure we really were on solid snow and ice, the pilots kept the rotors going, ready to lift off at the slightest sign that the snow was not holding.

Sjur and I helped the Russians unload six barrels of fuel. We had assumed that they wanted to reduce weight before flying closer to the wall, but Anatoliy signalled to Sjur and me to follow him on foot in the direction of Ulvetanna. At first, I thought he wanted to get away from the noise of the engine, until it dawned on me that we were going ahead to mark off the landing-place. Without a rope, and with fresh memories of

TOWARDS GESSNERTIND

the fatal accident on the Monica Kristensen expedition (A recent Norwegian enterprise during which one member fell into a crevasse and was killed), this seemed more and more foolhardy. The ground seemed free of crevasses, but then it always does, until you suddenly fall in! Nobody falls into visible crevasses. Even with Ulvetanna towering above us, it was at least five kilometres to our intended Base Camp. After two fruitless attempts we gave up trying to explain this to Anatoliy and plodded off with a panting Russian in our wake.

The sun shone down from a cloudless sky and the sweat was pouring off us. We were dressed for the Antarctic but this was more like the Sahara. Finally we stripped off our jackets, mittens and caps. Sjur surveyed the wall through his binoculars and decided the whole project was hopeless; the first 300 metres looked smooth as glass from where we stood. Suddenly we heard the sound of a motor.

'What the hell? it's that bloody helicopter taking off! Have those bloody Russians lost their minds?' Sjur knew about as much as I did about the Russians' plans.

'If that Jan's sneaked off on a photo safari and left me behind, I'll really lose my temper. I'll smash his balls with the flat side of an ice axe.' Sjur had been dreaming of circling Ulvetanna ever since he had won the toss with Thomas. He was scared stiff this plum would fall into the hands of the Swedish film cameraman. The biggest shock was when the Russians came in to land a couple of kilometres from Base Camp and started unloading our stuff. Sjur and I bore down upon them gesticulating wildly, but before we could get there, all our gear was spread out on the snow and the Russians were smiling happily and contentedly.

I grabbed Anatoliy's arm, pointing to the boxes and to Ulvetanna. He understood not a word, so I began putting things back into the helicopter. Now it was his turn to grab my arm and scream in Russian. I was too agitated to see the funny side. We were both yelling our heads off and waving our arms about, the rotors whirring madly above our heads. Finally I grasped what was wrong - the Russians were afraid of landing on sloping ground. They were uncertain of judging the gradient on the approach. Sjur and I took two of them with us and set off on foot for the last lap. We established our Base Camp as far as possible up the slope

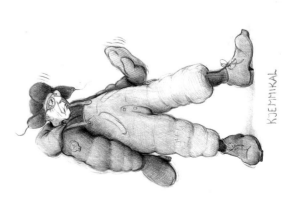

against the north wall, but at the same time far enough out to catch the sun eighteen hours a day. Half an hour later we had everything securely battened down and secured with ropes and snow anchors. We hoped to be back in a few days.

On the way back Jan grabbed my arm, shouting in my ear that we ought to contact the Norwegian foreign office as soon as we got home, and reserve the whole area for the world's greatest mountaineering adventure film. We would take our material to Hollywood and get the finance for a Big Budget film that would make 'Cliffhanger' look like Mickey Mouse on an ant heap. Ulvetanna had certainly made an impression on the Swede. Sjur also seemed satisfied. While waiting for the helicopter to land for the third time we had discovered two distinct, possible routes up the wall. One of them looked fairly easy. We dreamed of all the climbing we'd do when we'd conquered the wall. How wrong can you be?

Even on flight number two, the pilots objected to passengers on board when taking off from the ship. So Odd, Bård, Jo, Jan, Vebjørn, Carl Emil, Sjur and Thomas were all picked up off the ice, while the rest of us stood along the railing and waved. The return flight to

VIEW OF JØKULKYRKJA

Don't forget long johns, two pairs of thick socks, gloves, cap . . .

Thus far and no farther. The Russian helicopter took us to the foot of Jokulkyrkja, where we continued on skis the same night.

Torbjørnskjær was calculated to take four hours, the idea being that they were to come for us just after midnight. While I was engaged in packing most of my personal luggage, Erik developed the photos Sjur and I had taken of Ulvetanna, and transmitted them by satellite to Aftenposten, the biggest Norwegian newspaper. This was even bigger than the Americans' landing on the moon, (we thought). Our pictures would be blazoned across the front page in full colour. It was not until we returned home that we learned that the pictures had not been used at all.

At three o'clock in the morning the helicopter took off from the boat for the last time. A tiny flag marked the place where the others had been put ashore a few hours earlier. The ski track heading south was partially obliterated by the wind, but Odd and I agreed on which route they had taken. The sun was already high in the sky, but at five in the morning it gave off no warmth to speak of. The thermometer showed minus 25 when we shouldered our rucksacks and followed the tracks along the east side of the Lunde glacier. To the west, high rocks shone brown red in the rays of the morning sun, and down the middle of the glacial stream, we could see enormous crevassed areas. Our skiing forays out on the bay ice, surrounded by penguins and seals had been a fantastic experience, but one which by comparison now paled into insignificance. This was surely the most beautiful place on earth. Cold, pure and majestic. Peaceful - and wild. Quiet, but torn apart by raging storms. Inviting, but also treacherous. A continent of contrasts. My heart leapt within me and I turned - and saw the same pleasure and enthusiasm in the eyes of my companions. That was a wonderful moment.

'When did you lot get here?' Odd poked his head through the tent door, grinning because he had woken somebody again. 'It's already eleven o'clock.'

With the sun beating down on the tent, it was at least +25 degrees C inside, and I was soaking with sweat. The ones who had arrived the evening before were ready to set off, and we would have to hurry to catch them up before they had time to build a cairn on the summit of Jokulkyrkja. Dried milk, water and cereal; water bottles filled, and dried Knorr cup-a-soup with tomato and pasta. Down jackets, camera gear, extra gloves and snow-goggles into the

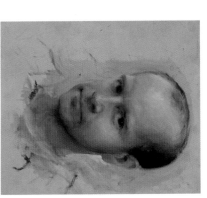

J A N   Å G E   G U N D E R S E N

We made camp 2,000 metres up, on the way to Jøkulkyrkja. Conditions were ideal: cold, clear night air and scarcely a breath of wind.

rucksack. I was soon ready to go. No sense in taking a heavy jacket in this weather. Biscuits and chocolate in my trouser pockets and 'blue extra' wax under my skis. The skiing team, who were to drag sledges part of the way, were already half way up the first incline.

We took our first break in an enormous wind scoured bowl over 2,300 metres up. The skiing party pitched their tent, and parked their sledges ready to continue east next morning. We were all in good heart, and enjoyed our lunch on a sun baked rock. Bård felt a bit worn out after the sea voyage, but expected to pick up now he had parked the sledge. We expected to reach the top in three or four hours' time. But the higher we went, the more apparent it became that all of us were not in the same physical condition.

Vebjørn, Jan and Carl Emil in particular were lagging behind, while Jo, Odd and Trond had begun to open up a solid gap ahead. On steep terrain every extra kilo takes its toll. I skid down to Jan, relieving him of his heavy camera so that Odd and Jo could take turns carrying it. That did not help much, however, and we were forced to stop again. This time it was Jo who caught me up: 'For God's sake, Ivar, you can't just push on ahead without thinking of what's happening behind you. Jan's got cramp in both legs, he'll have to turn back. We haven't a hope of all get to the top.' Immediately afterwards, Odd came up, puffing and panting. He blurted out the same as Jo: 'Jan can't manage another metre, the barometer's falling and I'm afraid of bad weather. I volunteer to go back with Jan.'

It was all very well for Odd to volunteer to turn back, but I was furious at our giving up so easily. Besides I was not convinced that Odd had judged circumstances correctly. True, the weather was somewhat more overcast than earlier in the day, but the dramatic fall of the barometer was due to the fact that we were climbing. I had been comparing charts and altimeter all day, and the fall in atmospheric pressure corresponded to a maximum of 100 metres in altitude, possibly rather less. When I put this to Odd, I was left in no doubt that I had less experience than he.

'Ivar, you've always got a mathematical explanation for everything. In the mountains, it's experience that counts. I've been using a barometer for God knows how many years and when the glass falls it means bad weather.' *For God's sake, Odd has no idea what a predicament he's putting us in. They're all convinced he's God Almighty because he's been doing this all his life. If he's got anything to say about the weather or the state of Jan's legs, then he should say it to me - in private, so that the least experienced are not worried even more. If we don't make a decision quickly, then the whole attempt on the summit will fall apart. I'm sure the weather will hold, and I think we should all try to get to the top. But if anything happens to anyone, then I'm in for it, having defied both Odd and Jo.*

I opted for a compromise. 'You go on to the top while I look after Jan. If he wants to turn back, then I turn back with him. If he decides to go on, then I'll carry his gear.' Most of the team objected to my turning back, but I was pretty certain that both Jan and I would get to the top before the day was out. Alternatively, I could take turns with Odd, Jo or Trond when they had already reached the summit. My sacrifice was not really all that great.

An empty rucksack and the ten minutes break for squabbling had given Jan his second wind. Several times I had to urge him to take it easy to avoid more cramp further up. Later on I we overtook with Robert who was sitting in the snow - and in a very bad way; headache, nausea, exhausted and with ice-cold fingers. I gave him my gloves and put Carl Emil's camera, which Robert had been carrying, into my rucksack before going on. One hundred steps - pause - one hundred steps - pause - ad infinitum. I simply could not make out why we were not making any progress. Odd and Jo were either tired out from carrying the heavy video equipment, or else they must have decided we should all keep together. For my part it was as much as I could do to keep up with Robert and Jan. My head was aching, I felt nauseous and weak. It was heavy going with one hundred steps between each break. *Your rucksack isn't all that heavy. This is just like the last few hundred metres to the top of Mt. McKinley. Can it be the altitude? Robert's never been this high before, but nausea, faintness and apathy all indicate altitude problems rather than anything else.* I recalled what Odd had once said to me on the voyage; that according to the mountaineering guru, Reinhold Messner, 3,000 metres at the Poles was equivalent to 4,500 metres in the Alps. I thought this sounded a lot, but even with something added to Jokulkyrkja's 3,000 metres above sea level it was no wonder we were struggling hard on the climb.

It still was not easy to gauge the exact distance to the top, but seeing the others disappearing out of sight ahead, we gathered that the terrain was levelling out. Probably we were about 2,800-2,900 metres up. Snow seemed imminent, but the visibility was good and the cloud cover high and thin. We were not anticipating bad weather, but with the thermometer at minus 30 degrees and no warmth from the sun, the cold could quickly become a serious problem. Most of us had undoubtedly drunk too little in the course of the day, and with less oxygen in the atmosphere, our blood was starting to thicken, reducing the circulation in our hands and feet. Jan's muscle cramps earlier in the day may have been something he had half imagined, for now it seemed to dawn on him that he was going to make it after all. He had perked up considerably. Robert, on the other hand was making very heavy weather of it, and was on the way to

The skiing party strove more than the rest of us at the start. They were to continue east the next day and hauled their sledges high up on Jokulkyrkja.

Later in the day clouds appeared on the horizon, but the altitude caused us more trouble than the weather.

losing all feeling in his toes. However, I kept urging everybody on. Robert would regret it tomorrow if he turned back now. In any case, we had a small tent and a primus stove in Trond's rucksack we could use on the summit if need be. Nonetheless, for every centimetre of progress, I lost more and more strength and in the end it was a question of whether I was helping Jan and Robert or the other way about. On the summit plateau I was so exhausted that I had to stop and rest several times before throwing down my rucksack and embracing Odd. Gone were all doubts concerning barometers and tired legs. The summit itself was on a small ridge a hundred metres further on. Clothes and other gear found their rightful owners once again - and I felt rather more confident when I saw thirteen men in bulky down jackets and trousers.

In the early days of climbing it was customary for the first on the summit to name the mountain he had climbed, but Jøkulkyrkja had already received its name when Queen Maud Land was first surveyed from the air. If they had known that this was Norway's Highest Mountain, they would probably have given it a name more in keeping with the other names belonging to the Royal family (Queen Maud Land, Haakon VII's vidde, Princess Astrid Coast and so on). To us, who at 2100 hours on 10 January 1994, stood on top of the Kingdom of Norway's Highest Mountain, it was obvious that Kong Olavs Fjell (King Olav's Mountain) would have been much more appropriate, so that is the name we actually used when raising our glasses (actually empty film containers) of 'linie akevitt' (Aquavit carried over the Equator in a ship; a particular Norwegian speciality), brought along for the occasion, in a toast to a successful ascent. Kong Olav's Fjell had a majestic beauty no less imposing than the jagged peaks of Fenriskjeften. The highest point rose protruded only a few metres from the huge plateau of snow and ice at the top, but the view was formidable. To the west there was a sheer drop to this icy cathedral's jagged, kilometre-long ridge. To the east the plateau seemed to merge into the sky. To the north Gessnertind rose up majestically, filling our whole field of vision, and to the south the snowfields ran all the way to the Pole.

If only I had been clear-headed and in a state to have enjoyed this experience to the full, but the altitude had made me tired and muddled. I remember the four hours on the summit as interminable drudgery. Most of our sponsors had been promised pictures of their pennants on the mountain top. Fifty pennants, three exposures for each, using a self-timer and chasing back and forth to join the rest of the team, had the sweat pouring off me. The others, dutifully producing one pennant after another - were getting colder and colder. Thomas and Robert started on the descent without even having gone to the very top, and it was not long before several of the others started back down to avoid frostbite. An artist is not supposed to manage away from the big city's sympathetic little cafés, but Vebjørn was last man down. All day he had impressed us with his stamina and determination.

At an altitude of ten thousand feet up we became enveloped in thick clouds. The snow on the ground, the horizon and the sky merged together in a thick, white broth and one after another we fell on our faces. On the way up we had noticed a few crevasses along the eastern

On our way to the top of Norway's highest mountain, we had a fantastic view over the surrounding plateaux. In such surroundings, Man pales into insignificance.

We had thought that a first ascent of Norway's highest mountain would be a pilgrimage toward the sun. Instead it turned out to be a cold and arduous journey, demanding the utmost of every one of us.

side of the last, snow-covered slope. We kept well to the west trying to avoid these crevasses, with the result that the journey down was extra steep and the long slope extra long. I was still exhausted, and it seemed an eternity before my skis began to glide of their own accord. When I finally drew up outside Odd, Jo and Bård's tent, my calves and ankles felt like lead after all that ploughing and turning on hard snow. Sjur and Erik, who had been ahead of Vebjørn and myself, had already fortified themselves with a drop of whisky and a bowl of soup. I was too worn out to go in and wish them bon voyage. Nonetheless, I looked forward to meeting them at Novolazarevskaya in a month's time. We envied the skiing party a little, because they would see much more of Queen Maud Land than we ever would. The idea was for them to complete a 500-kilometre journey on skis, skirting the southern flank of the Wohlthat massif, rounding its easternmost point before heading north-west and then on to the Novo base

When we finally reached our own tent we were all utterly exhausted, but relieved that Norway's Highest Mountain was finally in the bag. We immediately crawled into our sleeping-bags, having been under way for almost twenty hours. The Russians were to come for our communications equipment at twelve o'clock the same day to fly it to Ulvetanna. Erik, Jan, Vebjørn and I were to go in the helicopter and set up our base camp, while Robert, Trond, Jan Åge, Carl Emil, Sjur and Thomas were all to do the journey home on skis. On their way back they were to make an attempt on Gessnertind from the south west.

THE FIRST ON NORWAY'S HIGHEST MOUNTAIN

Jøkulkyrkja was first named several years ago, when Queen Maud Land was surveyed from the air, but we who reached the top on 10 January 1994, were all agreed that Kong Olavs Fjell would have been a much better name. So, when raising our glasses (aquavit in empty film containers) that is the name we all used.

Ulvetanna Base Camp

E R I K   S .   N I L S E N

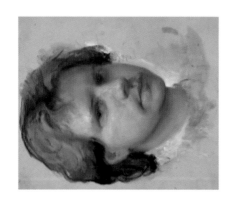

The sweat was pouring off us as we rigged up the base camp, clad only in our navy-blue long johns. Scorching heat like this was something we not bargained for. On the contrary, it was the thought of extreme cold that had concerned us. Thomas, who had grown up in a warmer climate, dreaded the cold. He had been listening to too many sensational stories about the terrors of the Antarctic. Partly as a joke, I had assured him that we would be able to climb in nothing but plimsolls and underwear which - at this moment - was strangely true. Being curious about the air temperature, I got Erik to rig up his brand new electronic thermometer in the shade of the solar panel. Imagine our surprise when it showed -22° C. The explanation, of course, was that solar radiation at an altitude of 1,750 metres is so intense that everything, (especially navy blue underwear and dark brown rock) becomes extremely hot when the sun shines. The dark solar panel was already hot to the touch. I hoped this was what would happen to the rock face when we began our ascent. Thomas' scepticism would then vanish with the onset of sunburn and sunblocks.

It was one o'clock when we landed and by five o'clock we had established our Base Camp and were able to phone home to Norway. It was our fond hope that the triumphant ascent of Norway's Highest Mountain would be front page news, but with the exception of a small item in two Oslo newspapers, and a few comments on the radio, our historic deed passed unheeded. It was a far cry to Mount Elbruz in 1992 when an Oslo journalist Arbeiderbladet fell over on the ice. Then it was splashed all over the front page under the banner headline: 'Vegard saved my life'. ('Vegard' was Vegard Ulvang, Norwegian triple nordic skiing gold medallist from the Albertville Winter Olympics in 1992.) All Vegard had done was to hold the unfortunate journalist until he regained his balance. Newsworthiness is hard to predict.

The next day found us busy sorting foodstuffs and rigging up electronic equipment. Even when we had set up the video editing table, developing apparatus, video compression box, two personal computers, a printer and a whole lot of other gear, there was still plenty of room for us to sleep and cook. Vebjørn, who had informed the female population of Oslo that he was setting off for the toughest place on earth, was almost peeved over how cosy it all was. There he lay, stripped to the waist, chatting over the phone to Mum and Dad at home in Norway. Dinner was bubbling in the pot while the latest pop music blared from the loud-speakers. It hardly seemed right and proper. Later, when the sun sank behind Ulvetanna, and the temperature in the tent fell to 21 degrees of frost, then everything seemed right, but some-how out of joint, nonetheless. Vebjørn grabbed the drawstrings of his sleeping-bag so that only the tip of his nose was showing, discoursing on how difficult it was to flap one's arms in a sleeping-bag. Gone were all worries about being *too* comfortable.

Despite the cold, I had no wish to go to bed. Yesterday had been set aside for transpor-tation, but yet another day without seeing anything but Base Camp did not seem quite right. Every tick of the clock was a second more to when we must return home. I tried to tempt Erik to a little night skiing to the small ridge separating Base Camp from the rest of Fenriskjeften, but he still had large blisters on his heels from Kong Olavs Fjell. I went off on my own after

Even in this fantastic mountain range, Ulvetanna was in a class of its own: queen of them all, steep and difficult whichever way we approached her. The highest peak in the Fangs of the Wolf, and overwhelming by any standards one chose to apply.

packing my camera and video equipment into a small rucksack. It was further than I had thought and it was half an hour before I arrived at the ridge. I approached the edge in a state of great excitement. Nobody had ever been here before me, nobody had ever seen what I was about to see at this moment. Ulvetanna's east wall, Kinntanna (The Molar) and the neighbouring peaks, were even more impressive in reality than in the photographs. I felt like dashing back to the tent and dragging the others out by the hair. This could not wait. *What if the weather was bad for the next four weeks? What if I was the only one who ever saw Fenriskjeften?* I ski'd back and forth along on the ridge, taking pictures and filming from all angles. Wide-angle to get everything in on *one picture.* I built a small cairn on each of the little knolls, naming them after each of my children; Mount Philip, Mount Nick and Mount Ninja. Subsequently, this whole area was dotted with little cairns after everybody else had got in on the act, naming them after various offspring and small nephews. Back at the tent I was as noisy as possible, trying to wake the others. I was much too euphoric to wait until morning to tell them what I had done. Erik woke up when I purposely trod on him, and in the course of a few minutes heard what he and the others had missed.

'Ivar, are you quite sure all these peaks will have disappeared by tomorrow?' Erik withdrew into his sleeping-bag without waiting for an answer. I sat there bringing my diary up to date until quarter past three. The sun rose over the ridge, bathing Base Camp in glorious morning sunshine. Inside the tent the temperature rose from minus twenty-something to plus twenty-something. *I wonder what all our electronic gear thinks of these violent fluctuations in temperature, and all the condensation dripping from the roof of the tent?*

The next day, 13 January, the Norwegian foreign minister, Johan Jørgen Holst, died. Jan heard the news while talking to Finn Andreassen, from the Norwegian television in Bergen. It

JAN PALMERS

was a strange feeling, suddenly receiving such sad news from home. We had already made a start on our first TV programme, for screening in a day or two. We now agreed, out of respect, to drop our original plans for a humorous programme and instead put together a short nature programme with quiet scenic photographs showing the beauty of the Antarctic landscape, supplemented by some of Vebjørn's paintings. Jan and Vebjørn spent the whole day filming, while Erik and I put on our skis and set off to find a route up Fenristunga. We were optimistic until we came to the hard snow north of Tungespissen (Tip of the Tongue). There, on peering round the corner, we were faced with several hundred metres of steep snow and ice separating us from Fenristunga. We slid down the far side across a great, big bergschrund and then ski'd back

Next day I went off on my own, Erik still pleading blisters on his heels. Again I climbed, and built cairns on five big and five small nunataks. Farthest north I climbed up a rock shaped like a perfect pyramid; The Pyramidskjer. From the top I had a magnificent view west to Gessnertind and Jøkulkyrkja, but no sign of any of our people. In several places the rock was so rotten I feared the whole ridge would give way under my feet, but the feeling I had when I sat alone on the summit made up for it all. Dead calm, hot, and with a fantastic view in all directions. Two of Ulvetanna's walls were visible, the north wall glowing warm and inviting in the afternoon sun, the north-west wall in deep shadow. Whereas the north wall was shining,

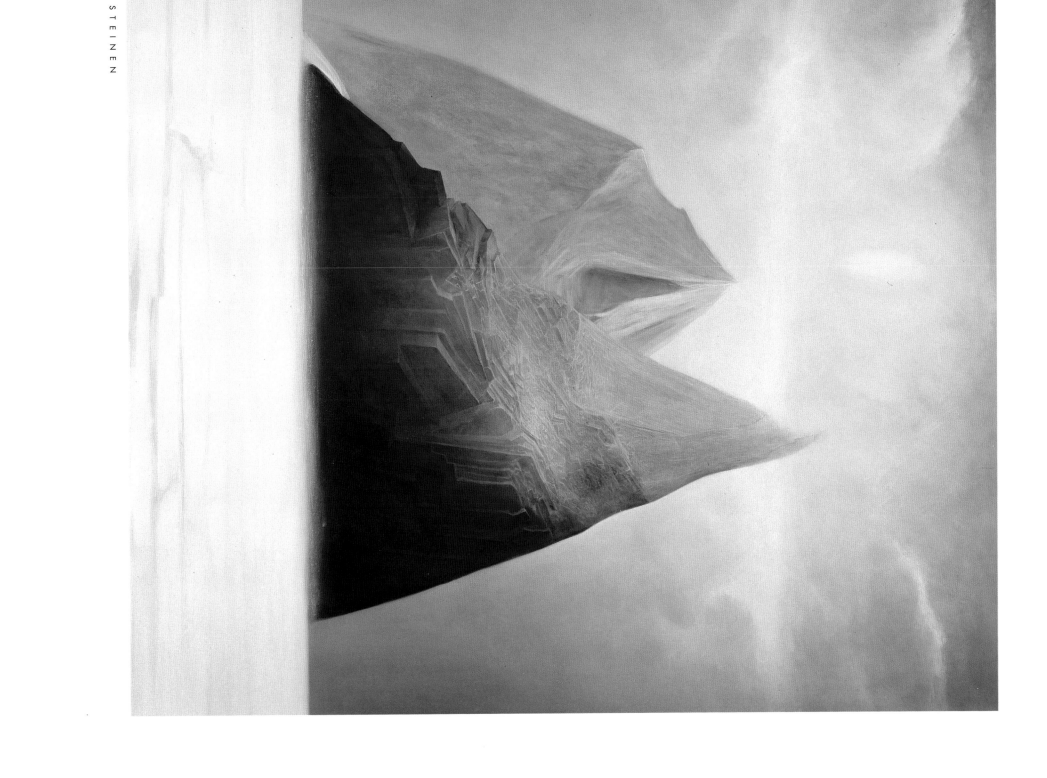

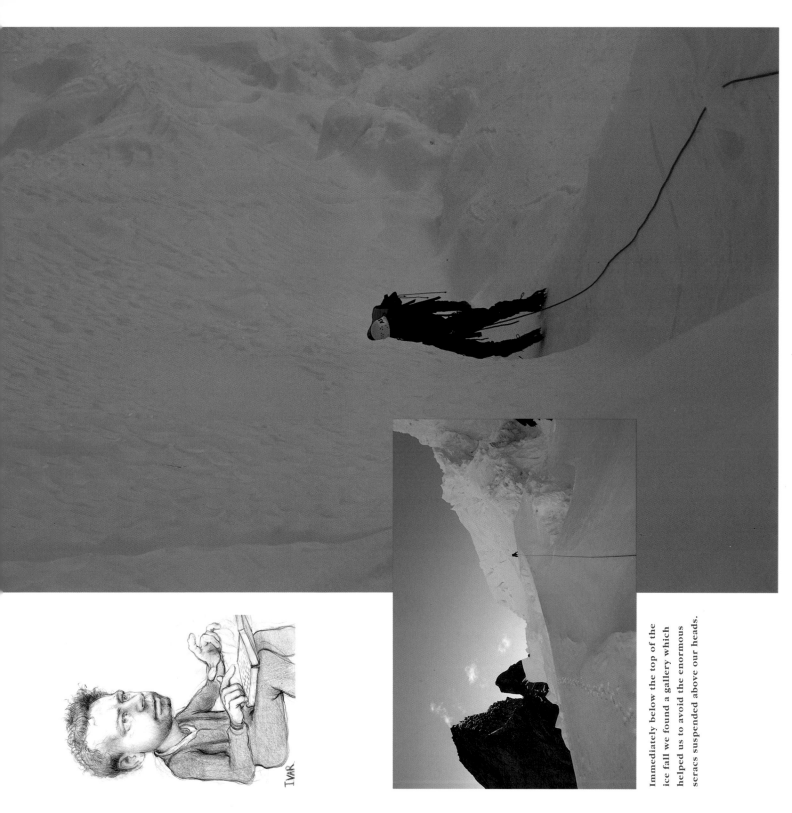

Immediately below the top of the ice fall we found a gallery which helped us to avoid the enormous seracs suspended above our heads.

vertical and warm, the north-west wall was ice-clad, tortuous and cold. The two faces of the Fangs of the Wolf were frightening, each in its own way. A route up the north-west wall seemed the best bet, but still looked far from easy. A rapid alpine ascent was absolutely out of the question.

Behind Base Camp, by the west corner of the north wall, there was a steep icefall leading up to Fenristunga. This was obviously the quickest way up to the plateau and the most direct route up to the foot of the north west wall. But under the ice fall lay débris by the ton, and daily there were small avalanches from the top of the rock face to the right of the ice fall. Nevertheless, after studying the ice fall with binoculars for several days, I was keen to explore a passage which looked relatively safe. Erik was glad to escape his ski boots and agreed, with some hesitation, to go along. Jan took his camera and tied himself into the end of the rope to take pictures. We found our way confidently over the first few crevasses, continuing steadily upwards on good, solid snow. Jan was not in a good state, but with Erik to draw him on ahead, he managed to keep up. As the climb got steeper and Jan more and more tired, proposals were aired about going on without him. But both Erik and I were keen to get him to the top, as all he had filmed so far was the setting up of Base Camp and Vebjørn doing some painting. Our ambition was to make an authentic climbing documentary - and for this we had to have pictures of steep terrain. The glacier fell into this category, but Jan balked at it and I was forced to belay him across the bergschrund and onto the snow at the foot of the wall, before we could continue. Here he could wander down quite safely to solid rock, and from there follow our tracks back to Base Camp. Continuing the ascent, Erik protected me with a 60 metre rope, but climbing here was easy; I only needed to place a couple of icescrews where the ice was rotten or where the going was extra steep. In spite of this, I became more and more apprehensive. Several times we heard nasty cracking sounds on the flank where we were climbing, and right above my head monstrous seracs threatened to crash down any minute. Not far from the top of the glacier I placed my last ice-screw level with my belt and buried the axe into solid ice just above my head. A kick with each leg and I was able to crawl into a horizontal gallery beneath the massive overhanging seracs. I had 15 metres of rope left and was able to make a fantastic belay ledge in a small hollow where the gallery ended. I was out of range of those threatening ice-blocks, but was unable to relax until, a few minutes later, I had Erik by my side. 'D'you reckon this is safe?' Erik sounded nervous. 'It's hard to judge, I don't like it myself. Let's hope we find a better way down. Once is enough for this kind of thing.'

We had been late starting out from Base Camp, and it was nearly midnight before we finally breasted the plateau. For the last hour we had been weaving our way through crevasses and narrow ice fissures. Safe from the avalanche danger or treacherous snow bridges, it was a pleasant tour on blue ice. A glance up towards Ulvetanna confirmed my assumptions of the day before, that the north west wall was definitely no easy alpine route, and the probability of its being climbed by us was small. In a bitterly cold wind, but with a fantastic midnight sun to the south, we crossed Fenristunga and climbed one of the teeth to the top. With the sun in our eyes we gazed south - straight into the mouth the Wolf. Its teeth showed up black and pointed, against the sun. This was Erik's first experience of steep mountains, and the panorama evidently made a deep impression on him.

When the Midnight Sun hung low over the South Pole, we climbed to the top of Fenristunga. Seldom has the mouth of a wolf looked so beautiful.

With Mum on the other side of the globe, all thought of decorum vanished for this lad.

On the way from Jøkulkyrkja to Gessnertind the boys had two wonderful camp sites out on the endless icy wastes.

When the sun disappeared behind Fenristunga, the indoor temperature fell from plus twenty 20 degrees to minus 20 degrees. Vebjørn's concern that those at home would think we had it too good dissolved in frost smoke.

Erik was the first to break the silence when we were down on the plateau: 'Do we have to go down that ice fall again?' I nodded. I relished it no more than he did, but the only alternative was to follow Fenristunga south, past Holtanna (the hollow tooth) and back to base camp east of Fenriskjeften. Without our skis it would take us eight to ten hours, and for all we knew we might stumble on large crevassed areas it would take an eternity to negotiate. Down the ice fall, we knew what we had to face - for better or for worse.

Everything went well until we had passed the ice-fall and I was halfway down the flank. Suddenly the ice gave a sharp report, and the slope shook under my feet. Ever since we left the plateau I had been afraid of this happening. The fear of being buried alive flashed through my head and I prepared myself for the deadly drop into the unknown. To be buried alive was for me, the worst fate imaginable and my pulse was going like an express train . . . then . . . nothing - total silence. The snow had stopped moving. Self preservation is a powerful instinct; above all I wanted to cut free from Erik, to save my own neck and get to safety on the other side. Instead, I stood there, whispering as loudly as I dared: 'Hurry up, Erik. Watch your step and don't fool around. One false move and the whole shebang's going to take off!' Without a belay or protection, it felt idiotic having a rope between us, but I started traversing towards the bergschrund, kicking steps for Erik whenever I could. Treading warily, then more confidently, we broke at first into a trot and were soon slipping and sliding unashamedly till we found ourselves on terra firma. Erik turned to me, letting out a roar of relief. Straight away the ice fall answered with an ominous rumbling, and at that moment the whole of the lower flank broke away. From a distance it did not seem all that impressive, but Erik and I nearly wet our pants. One thing was certain; never again would we climb the ice fall. Nor did I think anyone else would either.

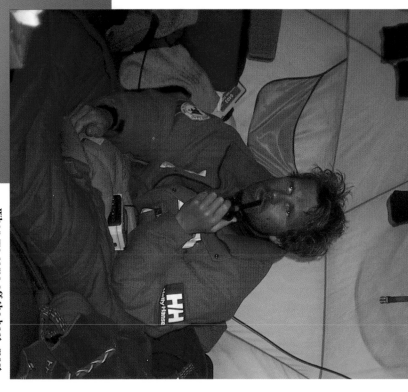

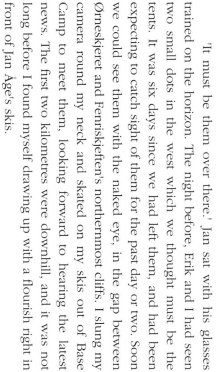

When we came off the boat, most of us left our cigarettes and tobacco behind. After a few days, however, we were pretty desperate and Vebjørn's pipe went the rounds every evening.

'It must be them over there,' Jan sat with his glasses trained on the horizon. The night before, Erik and I had seen two small dots in the west which we thought must be the tents. It was six days since we had left them, and had been expecting to catch sight of them for the past day or two. Soon we could see them with the naked eye; in the gap between Ørneskjeret and Fenriskjeften's northernmost cliffs. I slung my camera round my neck and skated on my skis out of Base Camp to meet them, looking forward to hearing the latest news. The first two kilometres were downhill, and it was not long before I found myself drawing up with a flourish right in front of Jan Åge's skis.

'Did you climb Gessnertind?' Judging by Jan Åge's broad smile, I already knew the answer. 'Sjur, Robert and I reached the summit three days ago - the night of the 13th. It was hellish cold, lots of rotten rock and the last three pitches were pretty steep. It took fifteen hours to get up and eight hours down.' Jan Åge was both proud and pleased with himself. Also Carl Emil was satisfied. He had been afraid of holding the others back, but in the event everything had turned out well. Trond, of course, hauled the heaviest sledge the whole time, while the remaining four had taken turns pulling the other two. Carl Emil was exempted.

When I asked Trond why he and Thomas had not climbed Gessnertind, I realized why he was looking somewhat gloomy. 'I wanted to. I thought we should all try for the summit as a team, but Sjur objected, he thought three should be the maximum. Robert and Jan Åge were the obvious choice as they were not going to climb Ulvetanna. Thomas was still suffering from blisters after climbing Kong Olav's Fjell and the others said Sjur had more experience than I did.' Clearly Trond was with the outcome, nor did he accept that Sjur had more experience than he, but he brightened a little when he continued: 'While the others were on Gessnertind I soloed up the Habermehl, and a peak in the same range, which I called Mikkelshø (hø = cupola-shaped mountain). Trond's son is called Mikkel, so it was not difficult to guess where the name came from.

Thomas hardly cared about missing the Gessnertind summit: 'I don't understand why first ascents are so important, regardless of the quality of the peak. Not to say that Gessnertind is without quality, but the route was fairly easy. My ambition is to do the hardest wall climb ever done down here.' True, Thomas had demanded that the wall team be the first to ascend Ulvetanna, but it was common knowledge that the important thing for Thomas was the degree of difficulty as well as the quality of the route. As we reached Base Camp, Thomas strode along with his eyes fixed on the north wall. Catching sight of the binoculars lying on Vebjørn's paint box he put it to his eye and inspected the wall methodically from top to bottom. Eventually, Sjur and Trond joined him, and three quarters of the wall team stood there for hours arguing as to which was the best route up the north wall. I had little to contribute, but found it exciting and instructive just listening to them. Just before the sun sank below the edge of Fenristunga, Vebjørn invited us to crêpe suzettes at the Penguin Club. Sheer delight, and with plenty of aquavit left over from the flambé process, a lively conversation continued far into the night.

Thomas and Sjur set off early the next morning, each laden with a heavy rucksack full of climbing gear. Yesterday's inspection of the wall had revealed two different routes. It looked as though they were making for the east route which started in a small dihedral and continued laterally to the right. They stopped for a while at the bergschrund at the foot of a steep snow slope, and as far as we could make out, they were belaying at each pitch. The slope did not seem all that steep, so we concluded that there was solid ice just beneath the surface. The plan was to overnight at Base Camp while we fixed the first four to six ropelengths up the wall, then

Ulvetanna Base Camp became our home for a month. We wanted for nothing, having two telephone lines, fax and computers.

With a population of ten, we were a happy little community.

5 8   U L V E T A N N A   B A S E   C A M P

haul our gear with a port-a-ledge, food supplies and other equipment to the top of the fixed ropes. With this done, all four of us could climb to our high point, clearing our equipment as we went. If the whole of the snow flank turned out to be so steep and icy that we had to use fixed ropes, then it might be necessary to move up to the foot of the wall the very next morning. We did not have enough rope for both the snowfield and the wall.

Vebjørn was up early as well, putting the finishing touches to a sketch of Ørneskjeret ('The Eagle Nunatak'). This was a very fine object which I had named when passing, thinking that the summit resembled an eagle's head. Jokingly, Trond and I had agreed to climb everything Vebjørn painted, so that later we could wander round his exhibition saying: 'I was there, I was there...' As Sjur and Thomas had no use for us on the wall, we packed a small day sack and made for Ørneskjeret on our skis. I led the first rope length and Trond the second. Erik set off after us, he'd wanted to reach the top, but in the end remained sitting on a narrow ledge half way up the wall. Trond had unthinkingly commented that the rock face was flaky and not to be trusted (which was true). A virtual novice, Erik was taking no chances. Trond's rope length, especially, was steep, rotten and insufficiently protected. On the top we built a cairn of large stone slabs which we broke off just beneath the summit. On the way down, we rappelled from a giant boulder which would hold us however rotten it was. Down by our skis, Vebjørn stood painting. He and Carl Emil had come from Base Camp together. Carl Emil had gone on alone. He was sixty eight years old, but still agile and every bit as eager as the rest of us. Yesterday evening he told us about his ski-tour from Kong Olavs Fjell to Base Camp and how concerned he had been when Sjur, Robert and Jan Åge were up on Gessnertind. As our oldest member, he had been worried about their being up there all night, but proud and happy when they all returned the next morning. He praised those of the team who had taken it in turns to haul the sledges, letting him enjoy himself unencumbered. Carl Emil could have been the father of Sjur (42) and the grandfather of Robert (22), but he was undoubtedly one of the gang.

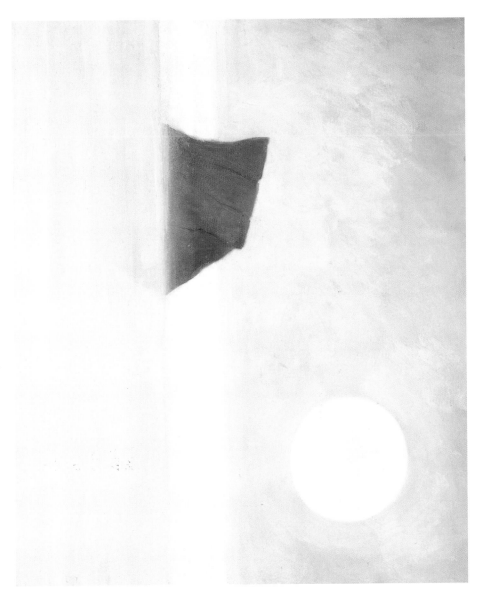

TOWARDS THE NORTH

The Fangs of the Wolf

In Norse mythology the Fenris wolf was a frightening monster, the son of Loki and the giantess Angerbodaj and brother of the Midgard serpent (who lies coiled around the earth) and Hel, the goddess of death. The Fenris wolf quickly grew so huge and fierce that only Tyr (the God of War) was willing to feed him. In his wisdom, Odin ordered the ingenious dwarfs to forge a chain that could not be broken. This chain was forged from the roots of the mountains, from the sound of a cat's paws, from the breath of a fish, from the beard of a woman and from the spit of the birds. Tyr had his hand bitten off when he put it in the Fenris wolf's mouth to prove that the chain would do no harm. During the Fimbul winter, three years without summer, the Fenris wolf managed to escape and swallowed the sun. The wolf now broke into the world with jaws wide open between earth and sky, thus threatening to swallow everything. Odin himself was eaten by the Fenris wolf and the whole world ended in Ragnarök ('The Twilight of the Gods').

After climbing Ørneskjeret earlier that day, Trond and I left Base Camp about 5 p.m., planning to ski all the way round Fenriskjeften during the night. Gone were thoughts of Ragnarök and the Fimbul winter. The sun was still high in the sky, warming our faces. We soon passed the small rock ridge from which I had gazed southwards along the peaks of Fenriskjeften on the first night. An exhilarating downhill run found us on the flat Sigyn glacier with Ulvetanna on our right. The east wall would undoubtedly be hardest. Compared to the north wall it was much colder, more exposed to the wind, overhanging at the start, without any visible formations, at least 200 metres higher and bare of snow on the rock face. If one icy kilometre overhang sounds bad enough, then lack of snow is even worse. With no hope of finding water on the wall, it would have to be hauled up. An attempt under extreme conditions could easily take about a month. Four men need at least 360 litres of water a month. This, in addition to all the other equipment, would mean hauling half a ton up an almost vertical kilometre. A formidable task which would soon exhaust a climbing team both physically and mentally. Perhaps Ulvetanna's east wall will succumb one day in the distant future, when Spiderman jumps out of the comic strips, but until then the east wall defies us all.

No human being had ever set foot in this terrain before, and the sense of being part of the saga of exploration was overwhelming. It was hard to understand why this, the world's most beautiful mountain range, had remained unexplored until now. Suddenly the thought struck me: *Ought we not to turn back? What if we were to let this part of the world remain untouched? Just think, if nobody had flown over this place thirty-five years ago, but instead had left a large blank space on the map with these words in block letters: FENRISKJEFTEN - UNCHAR-TED AND UNEXPLORED. How marvellous that would have been.* Alas, the train had already left the station. Fenriskjeften was still virgin ice and snow, but photographs and maps had been produced long ago. They were not exactly detailed, but enough to give us some idea, enough to spark off a dream three years ago, and enough to make me recognize Kinntanna's church-spire profile to the south west of where we stood. Between Ulvetanna and Kinntanna, 'The Fangs of the Wolf' and 'The Molar', stood two more unnamed and majestic peaks. The

On the way south along Fenriskjeften with Ulvetanna's east wall in the foreground, further back: Hel, Stetind and Kinntanna.

southernmost we named Stetind, after the queen of the Northern Norwegian mountains. Both had the same characteristic flat top. A few days later, after Jan Age's and Robert's dramatic climb, the lower peak was dubbed Hel.

Our camera was insatiable, eating up one spool after another. A whole film per kilometre on the way to Kinntanna promised well for this book, but boded ill for the remainder of the tour. With thirty kilometres still to go and only ten films left for transparencies, we had to impose rationing. Hereafter, each film had to last three kilometres, i.e. one exposure every 100 metres. Withdrawal symptoms tormented me; it was all I could do to keep my finger off the button.

The last kilometre saw us climbing steadily upwards to the top of the gully on solid ice. Our skis were unable to get a grip. With Mundlauga ('The Froth at the Mouth') to the south, we had abandoned the idea of 'The Tour of Fenriskjeften', but we did not take the risk of stumbling on the intricate crevassed regions which we expected south of Mundlauga. Even now we were having to struggle over treacherous snow bridges spanning sinister open chasms. Trond had his ice axe ready throughout the whole ascent. We had no aerial photographs of the area and looked ahead expectantly as the terrain flattened out and the horizon rose up in front of us. Most impressive of all was the red brown south wall of Holtanna ('The Hollow Tooth,') glowing mirror-smooth in the midnight sun. An impossible prospect. More than 700 metres of almost hand-polished rock face. A fantastic slippery pillar with lines and form more beautiful than anything seen in a sculptured monolith. Lower than Ulvetanna, but with cleaner lines, it looked just as imposing. To the north the pillar sloped down to a ridge which did not look too difficult, while the northern peak seemed little more than a steep scramble.

T R O N D   H I L D E

To the west lay Kong Olavs Fjell and Gessnertind, 60 kilometres away, but seemingly much closer in the clear, cold air. Trond and I shared a packet of biscuits and a chocolate crunch and put on extra clothes. It would soon be midnight and the sun was not nearly as warm as it had been a few hours ago. A biting wind from the west and a temperature of -25° forced an immediate departure. We ski'd swiftly down to Fenristunga and then headed north west at a fast pace to keep warm. Trond had no snow gaiters, and feared for his toes, while I feared I had been taking too few photos. I soon made up for it, but by then Trond was almost out of sight. For a moment I was a little uneasy. I was uneasy at being alone where I had difficulty

In old Norse mythology, Midgard was the home of mankind, and this was the name we gave to this ancient bastion furthest south in the row of the wolf's sharp teeth.

keeping warm, where nobody ever came, where the Fenris wolf roamed and where a seductive snowscape might conceal deep, mortally dangerous crevasses. Stuffing my camera in my rucksack, I strode out to overtake Trond. Slowly but surely warmth returned to my frozen limbs, and as I approached Trond, insecurity and fear of the unknown subsided. Trond stopped and turned as I caught up with him. 'Ivar,' he said, 'have you ever really looked at Ulvetanna's north west wall? If the alpine team can climb that in two days I'll never grudge them the top. Incredible how difficult it seems to be from all sides. I wonder if there's any other mountain in the world just as difficult from all sides.'

This was the same conclusion Erik and I had drawn while standing on top of Tungespissen. Was Ulvetanna too difficult? We had taken it for granted there would be an easy route up the back, should the north wall defeat us, but Trond had now confirmed that there was no easy way up at all. The lower part of the north west wall was festooned with snow and ice. This meant it was much colder than the north wall; so cold, perhaps, that it might be impossible to climb.

While crossing the back of the throat of the Fenris Wolf, we could see the tip of its blood red tongue, pointing skywards

Ivar Erik Tollefsen

Holtanna changed in appearance and character as we moved through the gap.

The eerie majesty of the characteristic formations of Fenriskjeften - 'The Jaws of the Fenris Wolf'.

THE FANGS OF THE WOLF

tinted by the midnight sun. On either side of the tongue was a set of teeth that would make the monsters in Jurassic Park look like gnats. The jaws were misshapen after having gulped down the earth, but even the tiniest teeth, in the west, were several hundred metres high, and even sharper and more jagged than their big brothers in the east. 'The Jaws of the Fenris Wolf - what a marvellously apt name.

A few kilometres ahead of us in the same direction as Gessnertind, we could see a fantastic medieval castle with innumerable towers and spires. It was a climber's dream - and a climber's nightmare. A perfect line of ascent, but probably so wide that ordinary protection would fail to do the job, and technically almost impossible as hands and boots could find little or no holds in the crack. With the Fenris wolf slinking around in the icy wilderness, we called the castle Midgard, the mythological old Norse home of mankind.

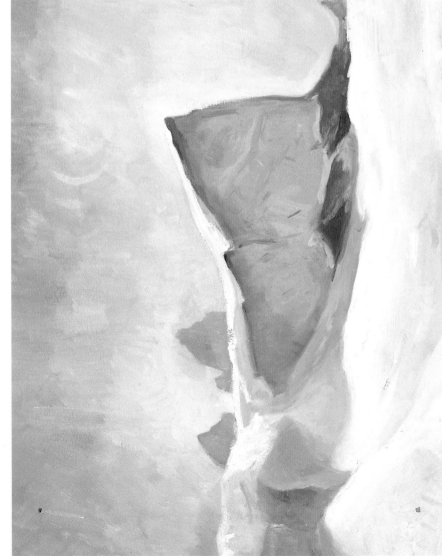

the highest point, passing all the different towers and spires would have taken an eternity. Halfway down the fantastic downhill run on the castle's north west side, Trond pulled up with a flourish, pointing to the most perfect crack we had ever seen. The bastion was divided into two by a huge, long crack that would offer 400 metres of almost vertical climbing - from the snow to the uppermost tower. It was a climber's dream - and a climber's nightmare. A perfect line of ascent, but probably so wide that ordinary protection would fail to do the job, and technically almost impossible as hands and boots could find little or no holds in the crack. With the Fenris wolf slinking around in the icy wilderness, we called the castle Midgard, the mythological old Norse home of mankind.

The last fifteen kilometres back to Base Camp passed in a daze. I was dead tired and Trond's feet were frozen. Every day at home we are so exposed to the media blitz of wars, famine and disaster that we no longer react. Something like this happened to us that night. The light and shadow of the majestic mountain formations were just as imposing as ever, but we were sated by the sheer mass of overwhelming stimuli. Purely from habit we might stop and take a picture, but mostly we kept going - in a hurry to get to Base Camp. Neither of us said a word when we turned at the last pass to look back at Jøkulkyrkja and Gessnertind. We had seen a mountain world without its like on any continent. And we no longer had any words to express what we felt. As pure as a new-born babe and as untouched as a clean sheet of paper. Thank God it costs a fortune to get here. I devoutly hope 'Round the Fenris Wolf' will never become a mass skiing event like the Vasalopp.

It was three o'clock in the morning when we opened the zip fastener of the tent door and looked in on the Penguin Club. The last guests had gone home and the waiters were sprawled on the floor fast asleep. Unwillingly, Vebjørn condescended to light the primus and make pancakes - so full of butter they slipped between his fingers, and so doused in aquavit that the bottle was empty after only one serving. No wonder people came from far and wide to partake of Vebjørn's crêpes suzettes. Vebjørn, who had never so much as fried an egg in his life, gloried in his position as specialty chef. The Base Camp tent was too big for a primus stove to provide much heat. The thermometer was still at minus 21 when we crept into our ice-cold sleeping-bags. I dug out my diary and tried to write a few lines, but had to give up - my fingers were numb. I was dog tired and it took me an eternity to generate any warmth. I had scarcely closed my eyes when the sun's rays reached the tent - and a new day had begun.

Vebjørn, who had never so much as fried an egg in his life, was proud of his new post as crêpe suzette chef. He even served his speciality at three in the morning.

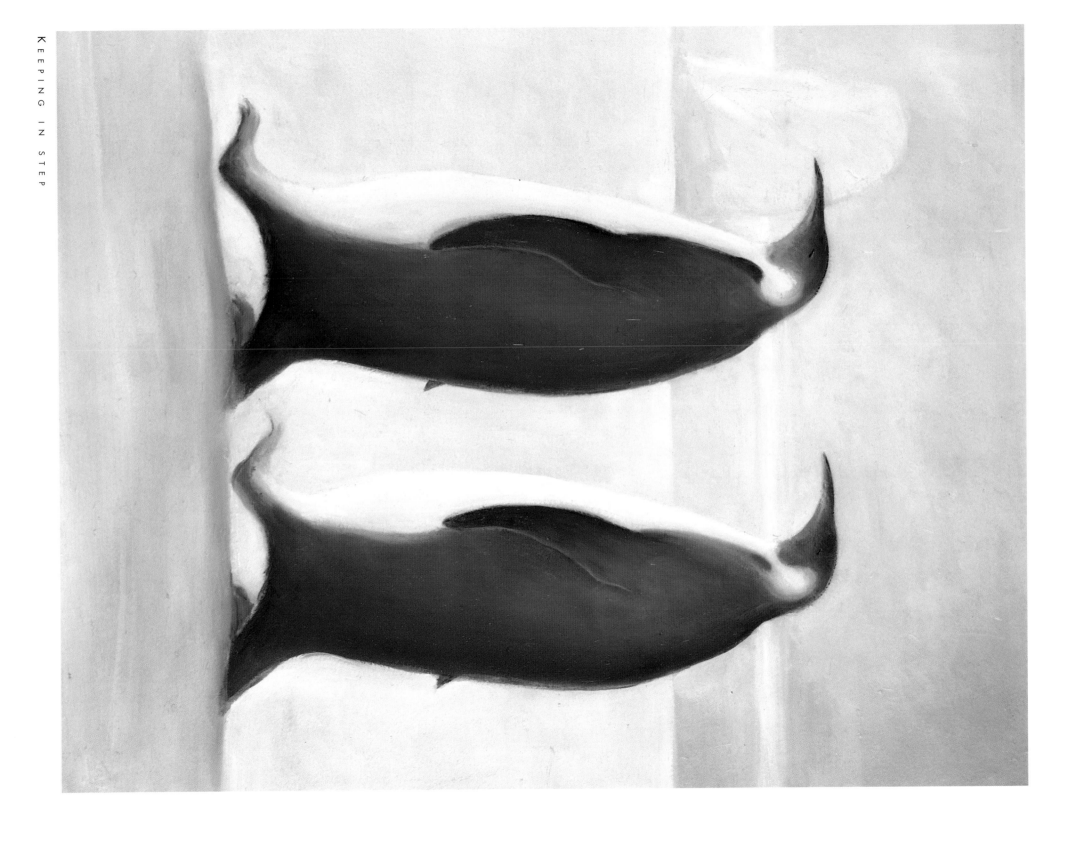

Steitind

Hel, 2335m

Ulvetanna, 2931m

Fenristunga

Midgard

Philiptanna

Tungespissen, 2277m

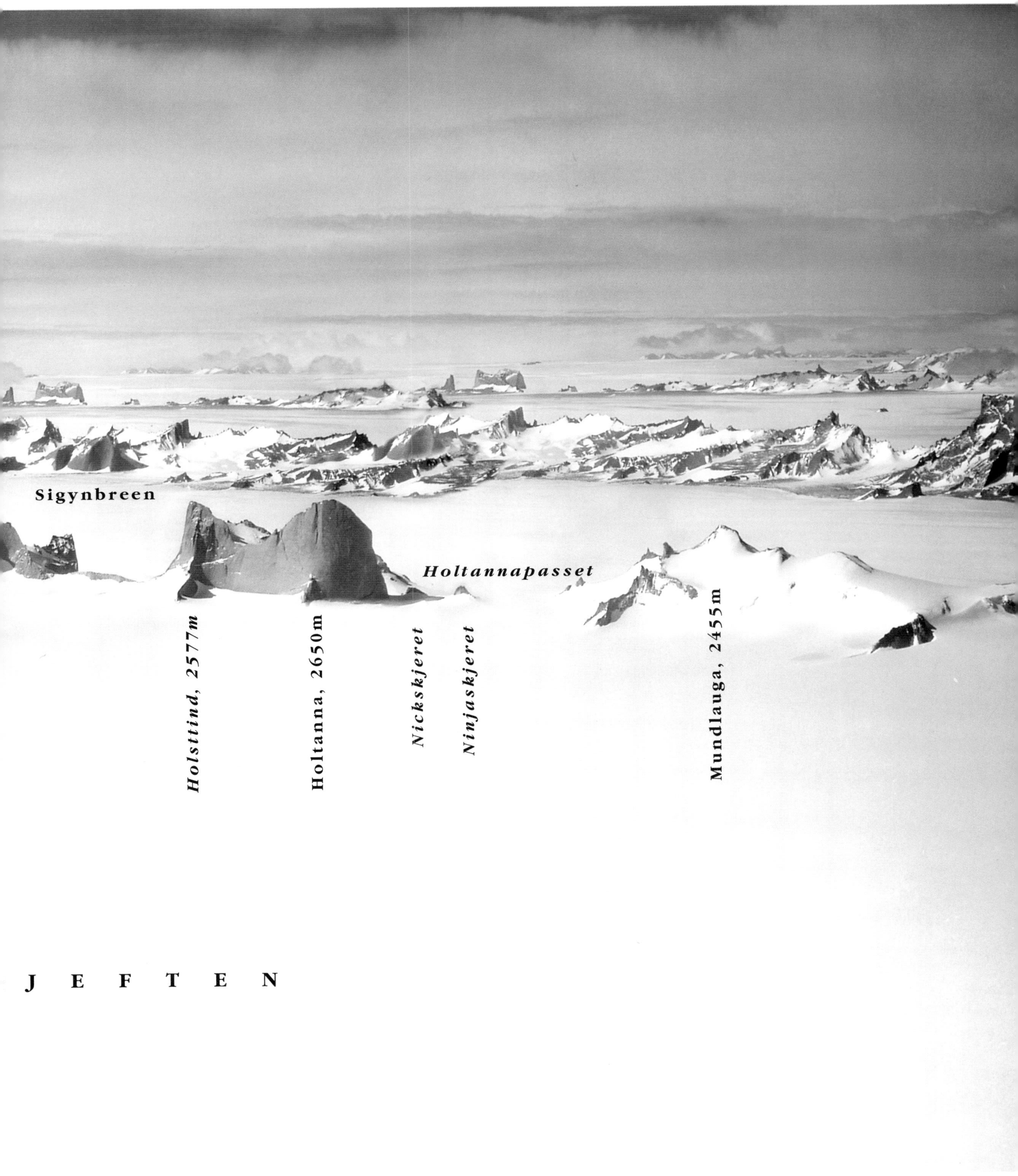

Sigynbreen

Holsttind, 2577m

Holtanna, 2650m

Nickskjeret

Ninjaskjeret

Holtannapasset

Mundlauga, 2455m

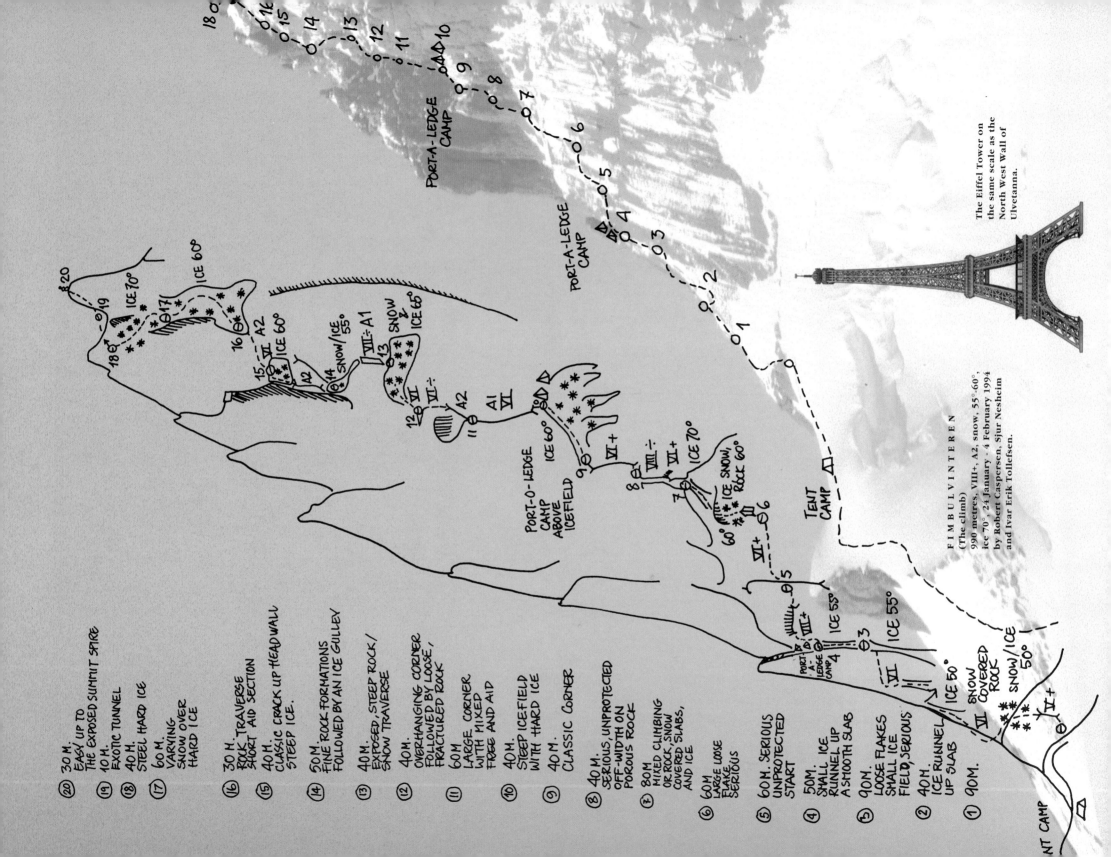

The Eiffel Tower on the same scale as the North West Wall of Ulvetanna.

FIMBULVINTEREN
(The climb)
990 metres, VIII+, A2, snow, 55°-60°, ice 70° · 24 January - 4 February 1994 by Robert Caspersen, Sjur Nesheim and Ivar Erik Tollefsen.

The First Ascent of Alvetanna, 2931 m

CLIMBING GLOSSARY

Aiders - Short ladders made of slings or rope used for aid climbing and for jumaring. Also called étriers.

Alpine ascent, alpine route, alpine style - Climbers carry everything they need in their backpacks. No hauling equipment or using fixed ropes or camps.

Anchor - An anchor placed into rock, snow or ice.

Angle - A type of piton fitting finger-to-hand sized cracks.

Bat-hook - A small, shallow hole drilled in the rock, which is used together with a sky-hook for aid climbing.

Belay - A stance at the end or beginning of a ropelength where one end of the rope is solidly anchored. Also the act of feeding the rope out to the leader as he climbs and bolting the rope fast if he falls.

Belay sling - A long sling used to connect together the various anchors at a belay.

Bergschrund - A gap at the base of a mountain between the ice and rock.

Big Bros - A pipe-shaped, expanding device which is used for protection in wide cracks.

Blue Ice - Solid, blue coloured ice. Usually softer than white waterfall ice.

Bolt-kit - Equipment for drilling into the rock, consisting of a drill bit, drill handle, holster, and bolts (which are placed into the hole drilled in the rock).

Carabiner - Oval-shaped (also found in various shapes) aluminium clip ring containing a spring-loaded gate which opens when pressed. Used primarily to connect climbing ropes to various types of anchors (protection).

Chimney - A crack or groove wide enough to climb into.

Camming device - A spring loaded, expanding anchor for use in parallel or expanding cracks where chocks will not set.

Cheater stick - A device used as an extension of the climber's arm for the purpose of setting protection out of reach of the climber. A tent pole is often used.

Chock - A metallic anchor which is set by wedging it into a constriction in the rock. Also known as a nut.

Cleaning - Removing protection from the rock.

Clip-in - To attach to a junior rope. Carabiner, etc..

Copperhead - A little blob of metal (aluminium or copper) attached to a wire loop. Pounded into a shallow crack or grooves where it smears like out cheating gum with (hopefully) enough force to support a climbers body weight.

Corner - A rock formation where two walls intersect at an angle.

Crack - An opening in the rock, usually where the rock has been split.

Crampons - Metal spikes fastened under boots for walking or climbing on ice and snow.

Freesolo - Free climbing without a rope or other protection.

Friend - A form of camming device used for protection in finger-to-fist sized cracks.

Dihedral - An inside corner resembling an open book.

Drill, drilling, bolts - Using a hammer and a percussion drill it is possible to drill a hole into the rock for the purpose of setting a fixed anchor. After the hole is drilled (typically 6mm x 30mm) a bolt is hammered into the hole and used as a permanent anchor. The bolt contains ring which may be used to secure a rope or other equipment.

Edge - A sharp corner on the rock. Also a small, sharp hand- or foothold.

Figure-eight - A device used to rappel and belay.

Fixed rope - An anchored rope, usually static, which is used for jumaring or rappelling.

Fixing - The process of establishing fixed ropes and equipment.

Flake - A partially detached slice of rock, often dubiously connected to the main rock face.

Haulbag - A large solid bag used for hauling equipment up a big wall.

Icefall - An area of a glacier which is crevassed and fractured as a result of the glacier bending around rock irregularities underneath the ice.

Icescrew - Protection which is screwed into ice.

Jumar, jumaring - Climbing directly up a rope using a rope-gripping device (jumars) which slides freely up the rope, but locks onto the rope when weight is applied.

Knifeblade - A short, thin piton used in very narrow cracks.

Lead - To go first on a ropelength and place protection while climbing. Fall potential is at least twice the distance that the climber is above the last protection.

Line - The route a climber follows, or wishes to follow. Usually the most obvious way up a mountainside.

Nut - Same as chock.

Nut-pick - A thin, 25 cm long piece of metal used to help extract nuts (chocks) from the rock.

On-sight - To climb a ropelength at first try without falling or hanging on protection.

Overhang - A section of rock steeper than 90°.

Pendulum - A technique used for moving between adjacent crack systems in which the lead climber lowers down some meters from an anchor and then swings back and forth on the rope until he can reach the adjacent crack system.

Pinnacle - A free-standing rock tower.

Pitons and pegs - Various shaped metal spikes which are hammered into cracks for use as anchors.

Port-a-ledge - A pyramid-shaped hanging tent bearing a rectangular aluminium frame with nylon floor and walls.

Protection - Common term for various types of anchors, such as nuts, friends, pitons, etc..

Rack, to rack - Organizing carabiner, nuts and other protection, usually onto a sling which is carried around the climber's shoulder.

Rappelling (Abseiling') - A method of sliding down a rope.

Rappel anchor - Used to anchor the rope to the rock during rappelling. Usually the rope is doubled through the rappel anchor so that, after a climber has rappelled, he can free the rope from the anchor by pulling down on one end of the rope.

Rock climbing - Free climbing with thin rock shoes on snow-free walls and slabs.

Rock shoes - Soft, tight climbing shoes with rubber soles for high friction and good adhesion.

Roof - A very steep overhang which looks like a roof from below.

Ropelength - The distance between successive belays, with a maximum length equal to that of the rope (usually 50m).

Runout - The distance between protection. Used as an adjective to denote long sections with no protection.

Skyhook - Used for aid climbing. A strong, fish-hook shaped piece of metal used to hook onto little edges. The climber hangs in his aiders which are attached to the skyhook.

Slab - A smooth section of rock, usually low-angle.

Slings, short slings and long slings - Short (25cm) and long (120cm) loops of nylon for extending anchors.

Snowbridge - A bridge of snow over a crevasse in the ice, usually formed by wind.

Solo - To climb alone, either with or without a rope.

Stance - A belay where it is possible to stand (as opposed to a hanging belay).

Static rope - A type of rope which does not stretch under loading. Often used for jumaring and rappelling.

Stem, Stemming - A climbing technique in which the climber adopts a 'splits' position to climb up an inside corner with one leg on each wall.

Traverse - To climb sideways along the rock.

FREE CLIMBING

Free climbing means that the climber uses only his body in order to move upwards: arms, legs, fingers, balance and smooth transfer of weight. Aids such as a rope and chocks are used only for protection in case the climber falls.

Grade I - Steep scrambling where hands are needed for support.

Grade II - Very easy climbing on low angle rock with many holds.

Grade III - Occasionally step and exposed climbing where good holds are plentiful.

Grade IV - Fewer good holds. Balance and strength may be needed.

Grade V - Necessary to find the correct holds, which can be small and require good finger strength, balance and smooth movement. Often steep and exposed.

Grade VI - Progress depends on finding the correct holds and being in good balance when transferring weight.

Grade VII - Very few holds. Requires considerable strength and coordination, together with regular training.

Grade VIII - Very sustained, difficult climbing requiring gymnastic abilities. Climbers at this level train and live as professional athletes.

Grade IX - HARD!

AID CLIMBING

Aid climbing is unlike free climbing in that the climber pulls himself up and stands on the equipment that he has placed in order to advance. This technique allows climbers to ascend impressively smooth walls where there are no hand or footholds to be found. Everything is allowed and, as a rule, necessary in order to ascend.

Grade A0 - Equipment is used to gain height, but aiders are generally unnecessary. The majority of the ropelength can be free climbed, with only a few passages requiring aid.

Grade A1 - Easy aid climbing. Protection is easily placed and is very secure. Aiders are usually necessary.

Grade A2 - Protection is still very good, but not so easy to find or place. Sometimes involves a few poor placements right above good protection.

Grade A3 - Difficult aid climbing involving poor placements which will support a climber's body weight, but not a fall. Some good placements can found during the ropelength so that the maximum fall potential is under 20 meters. One ropelength can take several hours to lead.

Grade A4 - Serious aid climbing. A fall potential of 30 to 40 meters is usual, and sometimes the climber risks hitting the rock or landing on a ledge before the rope can stop his fall. Danger of serious injury.

Grade A5 - Extreme aid climbing. Often no good protection can be found for a full 50 meter ropelength. Severe injury is likely in case of a fall, and the climber must have very steady nerves. Often requires a whole day for one ropelength.

Grade A6 - MADNESS. A5 climbing over a bad belay which can pull out in case of a fall. Certain death if the climber falls.

The North Wall

On 18 January we started on the north wall. Sjur and Thomas were up by six, and had already begun to climb when the first rays of the sun stole around the corner to start warming the wall. Trond and I had the day off, but we wanted to get up to film and take photographs. It was not far from Base Camp, but before we reached the bergschrund both of us were bathed in sweat. Holding the fixed rope in one hand we jumped over the gap and continued upwards. We followed Sjur's and Thomas' tracks and had no difficulty in ascending the whole snowfield unsecured, despite the fact that the last fifty metres were steep before levelling out at the foot of the wall. Sjur and Thomas had taken time to prepare the route on the first day, so none of us would experience any problems in getting quickly up and down in the course of the next few days. By the time we had started to carry up all our gear, the steps would be so safe that we could carry heavy loads without the risk of losing our balance. In practice this meant that we could sleep at Base Camp until we had used up most of our rope.

My legs were worn out along the wall at full speed. When we rounded the corner, we saw Sjur hanging out in his étriers, thirty feet up. They had started the ropelength with two small camming devices and a little chock, but had soon resorted to knifeblades, skyhooks and bat-hooks. Not exactly a promising start, but necessary in order for us to reach the cracks further up where perhaps we might do some free climbing. Thomas leaned against the wall, obviously pleased that at last we had started on steep and difficult climbing; the harder, the better. Soon it would be his turn.

In his younger days, Thomas had been famous as one of America's most daring climbers, the man nobody wanted to climb with; not because he was not a good climber, but because few others were prepared to try the routes that Thomas favoured. More than once he had thrown his rucksack from the cliff-top, parachuting down after it. That this was illegal made it no less exciting. Aid climbing was, for Thomas, the art of the impossible. As when he would balance between four skyhooks, so that each hook bore only a quarter of his weight, and then transfer his weight to the adjoining étrier, not daring to take a breath in case lungs full of air turned out to be a gramme too much in weight. Or when he had spent the whole day knocking copperheads into small niches, only to rip them all out in a fall which sent him plummeting thirty metres. Theoretically one can survive quite long falls (50-100 metres) as long as they are clean i.e. if the rock-face is vertical or overhanging, one does not hit a protruberance on the way down. At any rate, that is the theory.

'My arms are getting so bloody tired.' Thus Sjur in his thick Tromsø dialect. He had been toiling for four hours and he was feeling the strain of continually working with arms above his head. For the moment, he was stretched out on the étriers while the hammer clanged against the drill handle. After a spell without good protection we had to place bolts to prevent falling. The rock was as hard as agate and even using a small drill it took half an hour to hand chisel a hole big enough to take a reliable drillbolt. If things got worse everything would depend on Thomas. As far as work was concerned we others would be kept busy hauling, cooking, moving camp, mending gear and so on. But most of the mental strain would fall on Thomas who, despite all his hair-raising exploits, was still only human.

When we had finished filming and taking pictures, Trond and I returned to Base Camp. The descent was a bit intimidating at its steepest, but we gathered speed gradually as the slope levelled out, and by the time we reached the bergschrund we took it at full speed. Safely down, we stole a glance up at the wall. Sjur's white helmet was still in the lead. From this distance it was impossible to see whether he had made any progress at all. Trond and I went for a short skiing trip and when we got back Sjur and Thomas had already come down off the wall.

THOMAS COSGRIFF

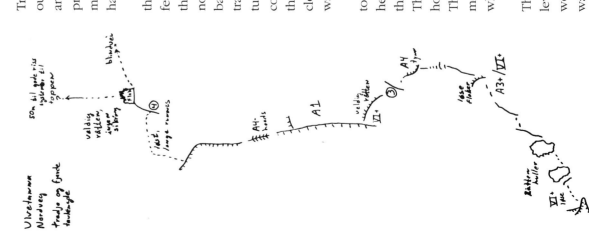

The North Wall started with a mild overhang, and climbing was desperately difficult from the start.

'Today we only managed about 15 metres - Eight out of eighteen placements were drilled. A bloody bad start.' Sjur was not particularly optimistic, and continued: 'I reckon two'd be better than four. It's such slow work, there isn't enough for four to do, at least not for some time.' Trond remembered Gessnertind, and did not want a repetition. 'If it's only going to be two of us up there, it shouldn't be you and Thomas. You did Gessnertind, so now it's time for a change.'

What looked like being an argument petered out with the arrival of dinner. For once I was keeping a low profile. Oddly enough, my interest in the north wall was on the wane. I was used to being leader and making my own decisions. Now I found myself deferring to Sjur and Thomas. They resented my leadership, of course, because I had too little big wall experience, but were themselves unwilling to set a course for the four of us. We were, for the moment, suffering from lack of unity and motivation; witness today's measly 15 metres. We should have been climbing in shifts around the clock. In any event the lead climber would be warm, whilst we others could use our personal body heaters on the belay ledge. But working in shifts meant pulling together and that was exactly the problem.

Sjur wanted to finish the first ropelength the next morning, but he and Trond overslept and a good part of the day was lost before they left Base Camp at ten o'clock. An hour later I ski'd east along Fenriskjeften. Glorious sunshine and a dead calm made the day the warmest so far. If I did not catch Thomas up, he was to wait for me east of Holtanna, but about half way I heard a shout and observed a figure free soloing an attractive rock face just under Kinntanna. In contrast to Ulvetanna, this rock was solid, with splendid formations. The sun was shining straight on to the wall and Thomas was enjoying himself in underclothes, rock shoes and bare fingers. We ate a few biscuits and drank a little U-nik before going on. Our goal was a first ascent of Holtanna; preferably the main summit but, if not, then the north one. We came too close to the wall, running into a patch of crevasses and blue ice. We left our skis here, a move we later regretted when we entered a bowl of perfect snow and finished up trudging. The downhill run would have been an orgy of long, wide Telemark turns.

'The ridge looks dead easy,' remarked Thomas. 'We might have time enough to do both summits.' He had been in excellent spirits all day and I returned his grin. This was sweet music to a summit-collector like myself. The glacier looked safe, but we secured ourselves with a double rope before proceeding. Over to the left we had spotted some crevasses, and wanted to be on the safe side. Soon after, Thomas broke through with one foot, but extricated himself without assistance. This was his first experience of a glacier, but he tackled it with his usual aplomb.

TÆMAS

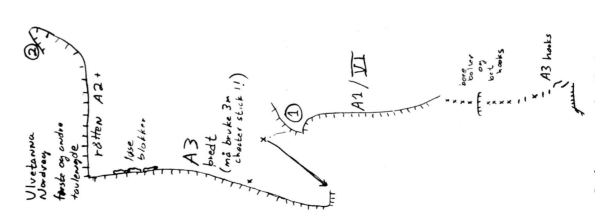

Ulvetanna
Nordvegg
første og andre
taulengde

råtten A2+

løse blokker

A3
bredt
(må bruke 3m
cheater stick !!)

②

①

A1 / VI

bore bolter og bri hooks

A3 hooks

On the way up to the ridge between Holtanna's sharp teeth.
Who would have believed that this
was the coldest, most windswept
and weatherbeaten continent?

Eagerly we left the snowfield behind, climbing an arête which joined the main and north summits. The view took our breath away - and so did the climb up to the main summit: Thirty centimetres at its widest, steep and slippery.

'Four hundred metres of unprotected climbing! It looked so easy from the snowfields below, but we should have learned by now. Nothing is easy here.' Thomas was exasperated. The north peak had looked like a Sunday walk, but it was with dark foreboding we followed the wind-tunnel along the rock wall. Twice we had to cross the bergschrund on crumbling snow-bridges before we were able to kick out a small stance. It was less than an hour since I had stripped to the waist. Now we were in the shade, and was down jackets once more. The altitude was approximately 2,450 metres with a temperature of between 25 and 30 degrees of frost. While Thomas slowly lost all feeling in his toes, I put on thick woolly socks and my rock shoes size 44. A few minutes later, however, my toes also went numb with cold. The summit was still hours away and we were forced to admit that once again we had underestimated Fenriskjeften. The fact remained, however, the north summit of Holtanna could still be climbed, given enough time and plenty of food and equipment.

Retracing our tracks we found ourselves face to face with Mundlauga (2,430 metres above sea level). Apart from a band of rocks encircling most of the summit it looked rather easy, but Thomas had had his fill of 'easy' summits for one day. When we returned to to our skis, we parted company, and I set off to climb Mundlauga on my own. After about 2,000 metres I had to discard my skis and use crampons. The terrain was gradually getting steeper and the friendly snowfields gave way to solid blue ice. At several places there were open crevasses, but never too wide for me to cross. It was when I reached the bergschrund that I had to search around for a place to jump. On the steep climb up to the band of rock would willingly have replaced my ski sticks with the the axe in my rucksack, but was afraid to dig around now. Moving from

I set off on my own to climb Mundlauga (2,455 m)

ice to rock was also delicate. Below me were 150 metres of steep, solid ice and overhead five metres of steep, smooth slabby rock with nothing to hold on to. After scratching around, I found a tiny foothold for my right ski-boot, which allowed me to reach over the edge. To make sure of finding the right way back I built a small cairn. Nonetheless, I dreaded having to look over the edge to locate the toehold. That aside, the climbing thereafter became more fun and varied, with decent, sizeable holds, but I was tired and took many breaks before reaching the top at nine in the evening.

With the sun in the south west quarter, the rest of Fenriskjeften was gloriously illuminated. Holtanna's south wall was an unbelievable sight, standing there, first in a succession of wonderful mountains. While retracing the route it occurred to me how different Mundlauga was from the rest of Fenriskjeften. Here there were huge piles of blocks instead of polished walls and the colour was a brilliant rust red in contrast to Ulvetanna's paler Grand Canyon hue. After a little searching, I found the cairn marking the way down. I put on my crampons and eased myself over the edge. My heart was pounding furiously until I found the little toehold with my right crampon and lowered myself on to to the edge of the ice. The bergschrund was easy when approached from above. A few minutes later I was on my skis once more. The way home was, as always, longer than the approach, and it was half past eleven before I skirted the latrine behind the main tent. Judging by the noise, most of the boys seemed to be awake and I was eager to hear news of the wall. I was taking my skis off when Jan Åge crawled out of the tent. 'Robert and I climbed a new summit today', Jan Åge announced. 'We called it Hel, after the Goddess of Death. Robert hurt his thumb when he was rappelling and fell 10 metres before being stopped by a ledge.'

Before I could hear the rest, Robert poked his head through the tent flap. 'It's a wonder

From the summit of Mundlauga there was a lovely view toward the north west. The south wall of Holtanna was an incredible sight, first in a chain of extraordinary peaks.

Robert was glad it was only his thumb that suffered when he rappelled off the rope when descending from Hel.

That piece of meat was well and properly stuck.

Carl Emil, Vebjørn and Jan outside the Penguin Club.

Postmaster Carl Emil preparing the cancellation stamp at the start of a new working day at Ulvetanna Base Camp.

I'm still alive,' he said. After a blunder like that one usually does not live long enough to be annoyed. Robert had every reason to be furious with himself, but Robert, and indeed every one of us, should give thanks to the powers that be for sending guardian angels to watch over us. *Thank God I'm not in the position of having to break off the expedition because one of the team has been killed. That was a close shave. Tomorrow Thomas and I will get on to the wall. I am looking forward to it and dreading it at the same time.*

Thomas lagged behind on the way to the wall. He took that as evidence that something was wrong: 'I don't know what's wrong today, but I don't feel well at all. I wonder if I'm sick. Sjur said that everything was organized up here, but it looks like a fucking mess to me. Why the hell have they left all three ropes hanging instead of one length of static? I wonder what it looks like when we get up to the belay?' With these words Thomas clipped himself to the 11 mm rope and began jumaring up the wall, which had a slight overhang. With a metre or two between himself and the wall he could not get a foothold and started to spin round and round, rocking steadily upwards. Everything was in my rucksack tied up in a nine mm rope for me to haul up when we came to a belay ledge. I had just fastened both jumars to the 11 mm rope when Thomas poked his head over the edge and shouted: 'EVERYTHING UP HERE IS A FUCKING MESS. GIVE ME A COUPE OF MINUTES AND I'LL FIX THE STATIC LINE PRO-PERLY FOR JUMARING.' *Poor Sjur and Trond. They'd been so proud of how far they'd got the day before. When Sjur had finished the first aid pitch, Trond had completed the rope-length by a combination of aid and free climbing. Before finishing for the day, they had hauled up all the gear, stowing everything, so that Thomas and I could get off to a proper start. Judging by the roars splitting the atmosphere above my head, Thomas isn't been all that impressed.*

We could just about see Base Camp from where we stood.

The temperature had risen by at least ten degrees and snow seemed imminent. Sunshine would have suited us better, but ten degrees of frost in a dead calm day was not to be despised. 'THE STATIC LINE IS FIXED. YOU CAN JUMAR ANYTIME YOU LIKE, BUT THERE IS REALLY NO RUSH IN GETTING UP HERE. I'LL NEED HOURS TO CLEAN UP THIS MESS.' Thomas was still on the warpath when I started jumaring up the static line. He had yo-yoed because the 11 mm rope was elastic, and designed for leading. The rope's elastic properties reduce the strain on climbers, belays, and the whole chain of safety equipment in the event of a fall. Static rope was un-suitable for free climbing, but excellent as working rope on a big wall. From that point of view, I had a more comfortable journey up the wall than Thomas, but exactly *comfortable* it was not. I struggled to synchronize the stepping and sitting movements, and used my arms far more than was necessary. Seventeen storeys up, I thought back to the year before when Thomas and I had climbed Trollveggen (Norway's vertical kilometre) together. On the first half of the wall I had been so nervous I hated it and on the second half I was so exhausted

Desirable Residence, 1.8 squ. metres with slanting wall. Just the thing for two people who appreciate a nice view of unspoiled scenery.

Aid climbing at the highest level. It took us nearly all day to traverse below the roof without gaining so much as an inch in altitude.

Thomas ran back and forth in an ever increasing pendulum until he managed to get a skyhook in behind the flake. Prodigious, daring and effective.

I got no pleasure out of the climbing, although I had begun to settle down. Even although Thomas had led every rope length, the climb had served its purpose. Henceforth, a big wall held no terrors for me. As a result, now I was able to enjoy the extraordinary experience of being suspended from a thin nylon rope in mid air, while I waited for Thomas to finish clearing up.

Two hours later Thomas had reorganized all the equipment, not necessarily for the better, but at least in his own way. He began to cheer up: 'It's hard to understand why they want to bat-hook all the way up to the flake. If you lower me off their upper drilled bolt, I'll try a pendulum over to the flake.' In plain language, this meant that I lowered him ten metres down, and he then started heaving himself back and forth in an ever increasing pendulum until he managed to get a skyhook behind the flake. Prodigious, daring and effective. The inside of the flake accepted camming devices and Thomas was soon

some way above the bolt when the crack widened too far, and our equipment no longer fitted. Five metres higher up there was a placement for a big friend, no. 4, but to get there he would have to use bat hooks at least five times. This would take him several hours and put too much strain on the drills, which were a limited resource. Thomas solved the problem by taping the friend to the end of a cheater stick, and forcing the friend with two étriers into the crack. First gingerly trying, then a more forceful testing of the étriers confirmed that we had advanced five metres in as many minutes, a huge speed for a big wall climber. And then we came to an abrupt halt. Not only did we have to traverse fifteen metres to the right beneath an overhang before we were able to gain height, but the traverse was extremely difficult and it took Thomas the rest of the day to get half way across. The pendulum and the cheater-stick had considerably reinforced his ego and he was in a good mood suspended under the overhang, pounding in copperheads and small knifeblades. 'It's quite scary, but it's nice too. I think we've done a fair job today, even if the vertical gain is no more than fifteen metres.'

On the descent I thought about our conversation while he was beneath the overhang, hammering away. Between blows he had told me why he had come to Norway four years before. 'You know, I was engaged to get married and came home one week before the wedding, when she said to me: 'I never wanna see you again. It's over.'

'When did you decide this?' I asked.

'It just came to me yesterday.'

'And that was it. No appeal. No discussion. After ten years together I still never had an ex-

planation. She just freaked out. I was so depressed. I started at school but after a week I quit and accepted this job offer as a programmer in Oslo. It was a escape to get away.'

To Thomas from Colorado, Oslo must have seemed like Timbuktoo; with eight hours' time difference, it was almost the other side of the globe.

Next day Trond and Thomas were on the wall while Robert, Sjur and I decided to climb Arnesteinen, an attractive twin peak 15 kilometres north of Base Camp. Besides Ørneskjeret, which Vebjørn had already painted, it was Arnesteinen which dominated our view to the north: two lovely pyramids standing close together and rising up 400 metres over the ice. It was named after Arne Hemmestad who took part in the Norwegian Antarctic Expedition 1956-60 - without ever having been on the summit, or even in the vicinity of the mountain itself. The previous day, Vebjørn had done a sketch in oils of Arnesteinen - thereby fixing our 'climb of the day'. It was still our intention to climb everything that Vebjørn painted.

The foot of Arnesteinen lay three hundred metres lower than Base Camp. Spread over fifteen kilometres, the drop was far too small for a decent downhill run, but enough to speed us on our way, so that we arrived after an hour or so. When we turned to look back at Ulvetanna we had a surprise. From Base Camp it had looked imposing but dumpy - but from this distance it was graceful and tall, with a summit pyramid like the Empire State Building. It had never occurred to us how distorted a picture we had had of Ulvetanna, believing that the summit pyramid comprised a third of the whole, whereas in reality it turned out to be about one half. For once, I was the first to connect what we now saw with our line on the north wall. 'We can forget the idea of leaving the port-a-ledges at the foot of the pyramid -and do a flash ascent in the course of a day or so,' I said. 'It is utopian to believe that we can manage the upper half of the wall in one day when it has taken us two days for every fifty metres on the lower half, is nothing short of Utopian. At the rate we're going now we'll be hard put to reach the top before the Russians come for us.'

Sjur looked worried. 'Do you know when the Russians are coming?' he asked.

'The answer to that is the same as before. The boat sails from Novo about 10 February. At the worst it will arrive two days early and should the Russians jib at driving their tractors right up to Base Camp, we'll find ourselves hauling a ton of equipment 50-60 kilometres. Maybe we'll have to depart Base Camp as early as 1 or 2 February. At best, they'll come for us on the 10th owing to the boat being delayed. The best bet is probably some time between the 5th. and 6th. Leaving out today, that gives us 14-15 days to finish the climb, and with the speed so far, that's cutting it fine.'

My own reasoning articulated what had been building up in my subconscious: *Perhaps we will have to return home without having climbed Ulvetanna? Ostensibly had been the first ascent of Kong Olavs Fjell which had been our first priority. But for all us climbers, Ulvetanna was first in our hearts. Ulvetanna represented a unique opportunity for the first ascent of magnificent mountain where every side presented a challenge. Probably one of the most challenging in the world. It is stupid to be on a pleasant little excursion to Arnesteinen when Ulvetanna*

From Base Camp the summit pillar of Ulvetanna looked squat and simple, but the view from Arnesteinen told a different story. Here it plainly resembled the top of the Empire State Building - but three times as high.

remains unconquered. If Thomas is so insistent that there should only be two men on the wall, then we others ought to consider something else. The north west wall is horribly cold, but I can cope with the cold much better than I can cope with difficult aid climbing.

My thoughts were rudely interrupted when the rope landed on my rucksack. Sjur wanted to film, so I took my turn leading. Two ropelengths later it was evident that the route we had chosen would not get us to the top. While we were fixing our rappels, I ventured to air the thought of dividing the wall team into two. I had expected a stream of anguished protests, but to my surprise Sjur more or less agreed. 'I've been thinking the same thing myself. For the sake of the whole expedition we ought to give reaching the top first priority, instead of an ego trip on the north wall.' Robert had no say in the matter, not being a member of the wall team, but he was not exactly satisfied with the way things had been going either. 'Jan Åge and I made great plans on the boat,' he said, 'but down here we haven't a chance to do any proper climbing on our own.' Between the lines, he was hoping that dividing the team would result in an extra place on one of the Ulvetanna teams; preferably with Thomas and Sjur on the north wall, but maybe I could persuade him to join me on the north-west wall. It would not be easy to tempt Sjur away from the north wall, even although his experience was best suited to the north-west wall's conglomeration of snow, ice and sheer rock. *If we do split up, it will probably be Trond, Robert, Jan Åge and I who end up on the north west wall. I was wrong.*

It was night before we got back to Base Camp. We had not discussed splitting up any further, but once inside the tent I presented my views to Trond and Thomas. Thomas said: 'It's fine with me if you want to split the team. The way we're climbing at the moment, there's no need for more than two. Trond and I have just completed the second ropelength today, and we will continue tomorrow.' With hindsight, it seems incredible that it only took three sentences to divide the wall team - and with no sign of disagreement. On board the boat every least thing had been the subject of lengthy and exhaustive discussions. The fact is that when we went to bed, I had not grasped that we had come to a conclusion. At any rate I did not understand that Sjur was willing to relinquish his place on the wall, but next morning, he and Robert had already started packing when I stuck my head out. Everything had fallen into place during the night. Thomas had the two man team he had been hankering after and Ulvetanna was to be attempted from two sides.

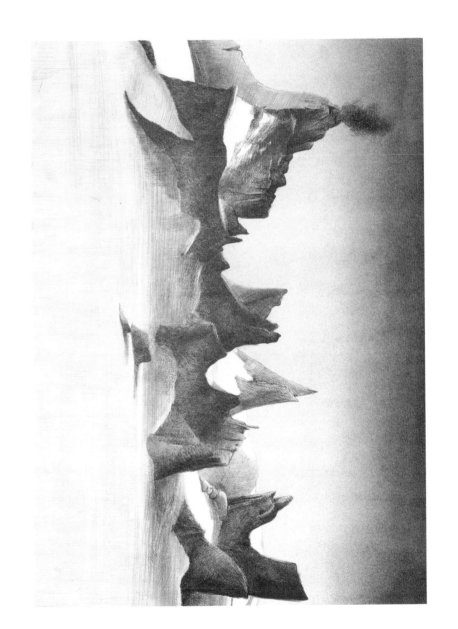

The Most Impressive Mountain I have Ever Seen

Long hard days were our aim. Together we would fight our way to the top. Sjur was to lead the uninviting ropelengths, those with snow, ice and rock - those where it was hard to find decent holds, and where his experience from 20 years of winter climbing would come into its own. Robert was our rock face expert: Norwegian national sports climbing champion, who could do a grade VIII on sight. He was the one with the fire of youth balanced by a maturity beyond his years who would be let loose on the last 300 vertical metres to Ulvetanna's summit. My job was to keep us motivated and going at all times, making sure there were no rest-days. I was the worst climber, and the worst slave-driver. I wanted to lead on the route, but had to accept that the others were better qualified.

I had forgotten how heavy it is hauling a sledge along. One hundred and ten kilos of food and climbing gear is like dragging wife and three children after you. After nine hours' exhausting grind it was all we could do to straighten up when we stopped. An ordinary crossing of Greenland is flat as a pancake all the way, but here it was undulating terrain and heavy going. The plan was to reach the foot of the wall before we pitched camp, but at the bottom of the last slopes we were forced to give up. Thus far, and no farther. Only a kilometre away lay Vebjørn's and Jan's tent. They had set off later, and arrived earlier. They had chosen the pass between Stetind and Hel, and were gloating endlessly over the amateur's total victory. They were not less overbearing when I had to borrow their shovel. I had left ours behind at Base Camp.

It was nice with only three men in one small tent. Base Camp was much too big and busy. There the will to work was swallowed up by pancakes, aquavit and satellite telephones. We had spent the previous day in packing and dividing the gear. Thomas and Sjur squabbled unceasingly over every carabiner, drillbolt or friend. Sjur argued as best he could in Tromsø-English: 'I feel this is gonna be a hard alpine wall. You all agreed that an alpine climb is more dangerous, and we got a lot more opportunities to hurt ourself. We need a bolt kit at least for emergency. I feel I maybe don't get it without arguing very much with you.'

Thomas agreed only with this last sentence. 'That's right, you're gonna argue one hell of a lot. We'll be climbing a blank rock face up there. We want the best bolt kit. This is one thing I'm not negotiating on. Someone else has to decide.' I did not disagree with Thomas, but I did not like the uncompromising way he forced through his wishes. Nor did he like the idea of resources being removed from the wall: 'Why have we spent days starting on this, just to compromise the wall team so that you guys can do the backside? I think we have at least as good success factor as you have.' It was better to take a little less equipment with us, than to be told afterwards that we had 'compromised' the wall team, so I said to Thomas: 'We can manage without. I can't bear to stand here saying we must have this, we must have that.' Sjur agreed. 'You're right. It's a bit daft. We can take the old stuff.' It was better to be the challenger than the reigning champion. True, we were all on the same side, but there was no doubt that it was going to be a race for the top. If we got there first and the others also managed it, it would be a victory for both teams because they had a more difficult route. If we arrived last it would be a double victory to the wall team. Either way it would be a success for the expedition - and that is what counted.

That was yesterday, and today we were already on our way. This was my first night out in the field together with Sjur and Robert, but the feeling I had had since Arnesteinen was growing stronger. We were already a close-knit team, getting on well together. From previous experience, I knew that in a crisis, team work and cohesion would be a strong card. Outside, the wind had risen, but it was warm and cosy inside the tent and reassuring just lying there close together. Before I dropped off to sleep, I remembered what Sjur had said when he first saw the wall: 'That's the most impressive mountain I have ever seen. An alpine route of world class- at

SJUR NESHEIM

'That's the most impressive mountain I have ever seen. An alpine route of world class- at least at first glance, mind. It looks like bloody Cerro Torre. We'll do it all right, but God help me, its cold. We'll freeze our balls off.'

With heavy sledges, we dragged ourselves up Fenristunga.

least at first glance, mind. It looks like bloody Cerro Torre. We'll probably do it allright, but God help me, it's gonna be cold. We'll freeze our balls off.' I was thinking: *'I'm not scared of the cold, but I do dread all those nights spent sleeping suspended on a vertical rock-face, with one millimetre of nylon fabric between myself and one kilometre of empty air. Nightmares galore: ripped nylon, belays that give, ropes that break, benzine leaking in the port-a-ledge and a variety of other improbable scenarios. A storm or two is more probable. And how does one react when a wind blowing at ninety kilometres per hour heaves us six feet into the air and slams us down to see whether the rope will hold? Perhaps I am crossing my bridges before I come to them. Perhaps there are stances where we can move around without having to hang on to a rope?* I slept; and dreamed of white birds pecking at our ropes. Robert was climbing up to chase them away, but

Robert was our rock face expert. He could do a grade VIII on sight.

just as he got there the rope broke . . . I awoke with a start – the first of my nightmares.

Early next morning I went down to Base Camp to bring up a few things we had left behind. To be on the safe side I took an extra port-a-ledge back with me. Sjur's inspection of the wall the evening before had not revealed a single ledge, but from a distance Trollveggen had not looked like a camping site either, even although the possibilities of bivouacking were many. Through the glasses I could see Thomas soloing the third ropelength on the wall. Trond had been poorly since we came down from Arnesteinen, but the suggestion that Jan Age should belay Thomas had been dropped. It was still only twelve o'clock and Thomas was already halfway up. I felt the competitive goad, and left Base Camp in a hurry.

I overtook Sjur and Robert while they were sitting on the sledges, staring across Fenristunga. After I had gone, they dozed off again, not waking until noon. Actually we could have left the tent on the tongue, but by moving it up to the start of the climb, we could make certain of full time climbing. With rucksacks as heavy as lead we kicked tracks on the steep snow slopes, and after an hour's hard slog reached the most perfect tent site I have ever seen. A general could not have found a better spot to defend. Even a pilot would have been delighted. It was ideally situated on Ulvetanna's north west shoulder with a view in three separate directions: south to the Pole, north to the rest of the world and west to Gessnertind and Jokulkyrkja.

Gingerly, we approached the edge, and found ourselves looking 700 metres straight down to Base Camp. We had a bird-like sensation of flying. Through the glasses I could see Vebjorn and Erik wandering around outside the tent. The dark figure on its way down the wall had to be Thomas. It did wonders for our morale getting so high so quickly. Sjur borrowed the

We had more equipment than a well stocked climbers' shop. Even so we squabbled over every bolt and carabiner when we divided our forces.

For Robert, dividing the wall team was a welcome opportunity to climb a long and difficult route.

Heavily laden southwards over the Sigyn glacier. At an altitude of of 1,700 metres, it was still more than another kilometre to the the summit of Ulvetanna.

On the day we split up Trond fell ill, and Thomas' two-man team was suddenly halved.

glasses but could not manage to see how far Thomas had got. Having inspected the route winding upwards he pronounced his decision: 'I'm looking straight at their route, Robert. There's a gradual overhang from that grey hole and upwards. Not a single formation. They're never going to make it.' At the time I did not take much notice of Sjur's pronouncements, assuming he was jealous of Thomas and Trond, because they were on the most prestigious route.

Immediately afterwards Sjur began to lead the first ropelength. Our aim was two ropelengths before returning to the sledges to retrieve the rest of the food. Nobody was allowed to relax before the day's or night's objectives had been achieved. The first ropelength was a typical Sjur start with a stance on the lower lip of the bergschrund, a single good icescrew on the upper lip, then 20 metres nerve-racking climbing on snow covered rock without any running belays. The gradient was only 50 degrees, but the snow was too thin to give a proper hold and too thick to brush away. Sjur sweated and swore for nearly an hour before he discovered a thin crack where he placed an Alien and was then able to lean back on the rope and rest. The remainder of the ropelength was easier, but when the rope ran out, 15-20 metres still remained

'Tell Thomas the route looks pretty desperate past the grey hole. Lots of drilling and no visible formations. Sjur checked with the binoculars earlier on.'

The North West Wall of Ulvetanna was an impressive sight. Little did we know that it would be 11 days before we saw the shoulder again.

Ideally situated on Ulvetanna's north west shoulder with a view in three separate directions: south to the Pole, north to the rest of the world and west to Gessnertind and Jokulkyrkja.

The first ropelength was a typical Sjur start: Steep snow from the bergschrund, then nerve-racking climbing on snow covered rock.

to the edge of the north wall and a reasonable stance. Robert spliced another rope and offered up a small prayer that the distance up to the first running belay was longer than the distance up to the stance. When the knot stopped at the carabiner it was still two metres short, but with the help of a couple of long slings Sjur managed to secure the rope so that Robert could jumar up after him.

Hacking out three cubic metres of ice with an ice-axe is no small task, but I was determined to make us a proper camping site. With a clear view three quarters of the way round the compass, we were extremely exposed to the wind. I used all the loose-lying material I could lay hands on to build a sufficiently high sheltering wall. When I was half finished Base Camp came over the radio: 'This is Ulvetanna Base Camp to Ivar. Come in. Over!' Jan Åge was loud and clear. We chatted for a few minutes and he confirmed that Thomas had completed a ropelength solo. Impressive! There was no news of Jan and Vebjørn. Either they were out of range, or they had forgotten to switch on.

'Tell Thomas the route looks pretty desperate past the grey hole. Lots of drilling and no visible formations. Sjur checked with the binoculars earlier on.'

'Hi, Ivar, I'm here too. I've been up there today and think it will work. One more ropelength and I think we're OK. Over.' This was Thomas. I had simply reported what Sjur had to say and had nothing of my own to add. Intuitively I took it for granted that Thomas was right, and I felt how I became a little envious that things were going so well on the north wall. We arranged to be on the air again at nine o'clock the next morning.

By midnight Sjur had completed ropelength No. 2, and I had pitched our tent inside a commodious citadel of ice. The climbing itself presented few problems, but it had taken us some time to find belays. Much of the time passed in brushing away snow, or looking for cracks sufficient to take a piton or a nut. One hundred and thirty metres in eight hours was not nearly enough, and as the terrain sloped so gently the vertical gain was only half what it might have been. Our last stance was quite an experience. The same conditions as down here, except that the ledge had room for a pair of boots instead of a tent. As we made our descent, Fenristunga was deep blue and the mountains bathed in a golden glow. A magic moment. At three o'clock we crawled into our sleeping bags and nodded to each other, well pleased. In the course of the day, we had made camp at the foot of the climb, fetched all our food and gear, and fixed two long ropelengths. Tomorrow we would head for the big cleft in the corner. Perhaps there would be space for a small tent. The Alpine team was on its way.

'Are you quite sure you've been on a course?' Sjur was concerned about my flying a paraglider.

'Sure, both Erik and I have a licence. If you'd just get out of my way, I'll try to remember how to arranged these lines.' Sjur was not convinced. 'Bård tells me you have a licence for buses and trailers - but you can't drive either. He says you always know someone who can fix things for you.' I had to agree with Bård where trailers were concerned, though it was a fact that I had passed the test. Paragliding was another kettle of fish. I had had three days' practice and passed the theoretical test a couple of days before we left. Admittedly I was not qualified for a diving take off, but with a little elasticity in defining terms, this did not fall within that category. I had

At a frightening altitude over Fenristunga, I finally regained control over the paraglider, and began to prepare for a safe landing far from the thermals around Ulvetanna.

In seconds my paraglider rocketed hundreds of metres into the air, at the same time being sucked in toward Ulvetanna's north-west wall.

I was not qualified for a diving take off, but with a little elasticity in defining terms, this did not fall within that category.

tried a take-off on the snow slopes beneath the north wall without getting the wing up properly. The air was too thin and the tailwind too strong. This was my last chance to qualify for the sponsor bonus. Jan was ready down on Fenristunga with his video camera, and Robert had an open radio line:

'This is Ulvetanna Tower to Jan. The bird will be on the wing in 10 minutes. Stand by to film. Over.'

Jan answered in his second language: 'We read you loud and clear. Cameras rolling in five minutes. Over.'

The conditions seemed good. A white, mushroom-shaped fair-weather cloud hung over Ulvetanna's summit in an otherwise cloudless sky. The little wind there was, wafted against the wall. All the same I was nervous. Sunday practice in Norway with someone monitoring wind velocity and direction, was one thing. It was something else being 2,400 metres up on a mountain almost nobody knew existed. If I did not get my wing up, I would dive over the edge without a chance of stopping myself. With crampons and axe I might have had a chance, but had been afraid of hurting myself on so many sharp edges so I had left them behind. The ground was slippery. Sjur and Robert were crouched down behind, holding on to the wing. I hoped they knew how to lift the rear end when I took off.

'You don't seem very happy, Ivar,' grunted Sjur, 'you ought to drop the whole thing. It's too hard for your first time on your own.' Secretly, I agreed with him, but now I was ready for take off: Mountaineer's helmet on my head; harness tightened, not too taut around the thighs; a brake handle in either hand and a good grip on the front raisers, and a quick glance over each shoulder to check that the lines were in place. *Don't forget the start procedure. Run with even movements. Lean well forward and release the front raisers when the wing rises. Continue with the wing above your head, and carry on running until you are in the air. Brake a little for a smooth lift off:* I had never bungled a start before.

'Are you ready, boys?' Both of them nodded, giving me the thumbs up sign. 'Then I'm off! ON YOUR MARKS, GET SET, GO!'

The wing shot over my head and I was in the air almost before I'd managed to release the raisers. Fear of a dud start gave place to a new and much more frightening feeling. THE WING WOULD NOT MAKE IT OVER FENRISTUNGA! Instead I was being sucked south along the length of Ulvetanna simultaneously climbing higher and higher. Soon I had gained several hundred metres and found myself halfway up Ulvetanna. Dim recollections of theory classes informed me I was caught in a thermal, those strong, rising air currents caused by the sun's warming the rock face. I was nervous, at a loss what to do, hoping that the updraught would cease somewhat if only I could get away from the wall. Gingerly, I tried to force the wing out over Fenristunga. It dawned on me that something must be wrong when the wind got worse, and the wing started bucketing. The more I pushed, the more unstable it became, and suddenly it disappeared behind me, only to shoot forward again like a rocket. I panicked, pulled too hard on the brake and almost reared up. Next time the wing shot forward, I was ready for it and managed to brake more smoothly. Suddenly the blessed thing took on a mind of its own, starting to swing violently from side to side. I had no idea how to counteract this. Once again I panicked. *This is stupid. There are three small children waiting for you at home and you go and get yourself killed for the sake of a picture or two for a sponsor. Why do I always think it can never happen to me? Why am I always so cocksure it'll be allright on the night! Not this time though. One more whack and I'll go into a spin and hit the ground. Blast, blast, blast!* According to the manual, panic position requires letting go and allowing the wing act on its own, but I dared not do that. A mighty whack from the left slewed the wing halfway round to Ulvetanna again. I swung to the west, farther and farther out over Fenristunga with the wing flapping madly. Gradually the wind dropped and the air became calmer. I did not dare turn and try a landing at the foot of the wall, so I continued well to the west before executing a turn and landing on a gentle slope. Down! And still alive! Inwardly, I was jubilant, but I was sobbing with pleasure and relief, while the tension slowly seeped out of my body. My God, how good it is to be alive when you were sure you were about to die.

Trudging up to Vebjørn and Jan, I promised myself to take more care in the future. Perhaps what had happened had not been all that serious, but it had scared me all the same.

The last bit up to the cleft was an unbroken, snow-covered crack half a metre in width, with solid ice under the snow. Sjur made good use of crampons and ice axe.

we had a great deal of trouble rigging the port-a-ledges. The slope was too steep for a conventional tent, but too slack for simple use of the suspended variety which is the port-a-ledge.

Studying Jan's monitor, I could plainly see how the wing had been slewing back and forth and how it shot madly forward a couple of times. I was curious to know how it had looked to Sjur and Robert and with my body racing with adrenalin I galloped across the snow towards the tent. But they were already halfway up the ropes. A new day had begun.

Probably we would move up into the the cleft the next day, so I started packing. Normally, I would have reduced the weight to a minimum, but something told me it was best to have something in reserve, so I took all of the food except four bags of crisps. This was our only chance to climb Ulvetanna. It would be idiotic having to turn back for want of food. It would be considerably more serious i we ran out of fuel or the primus refused to function. I put in an extra primus and plenty of fuel. We had mislaid the kit of spare parts, but it was most unlikely that both primuses would give trouble simultaneously, or so I thought. With two port-a-ledges and five ropes I had to pack a large haulbag as well as three bulging rucksacks. The haulbag was a monster of over 40 kilos and at least one metre high. The terrain was too slack for hauling, so somebody would have to carry it until we reached the upper wall. There would be no volunteers for that job.

Through the telescope I could see that Sjur had finally completed the third ropelength, and Robert was now on the way up. The last bit to the cleft was a long, snow filled cleft about half a metre wide and most certainly ice bound beneath the snow. On ice Sjur would be able to make fast progress using two axes and crampons with icescrews for protection. Without ice in the cleft we would probably have to move out on to the rock with rock shoes and bolts. Other alternatives there were none, and it would take time.

Luck was with us. The crack turned to be the easiest ropelength so far. When Sjur and Robert came down again we shared a drop of aquavit in honour of the fact that the first stage of the climb was in the bag. Tomorrow we would move up onto the wall and I would experience my first night's sleep in a port-a-ledge. After sweating over it for about an hour, Sjur had managed to hack out a small platform where two of us could stand side by side, but there was no room for a tent. Having used up all his ice-screws, he had had to rappel down from two copperheads and an ice axe on our thin 100-metre rope. From below, the rope had seemed short, but with its 90 metres it was our longest yet. We hoped to wedge two port-a-ledges one above the other in the cleft, but there were few means of securing them. The latest from Base Camp was that Thomas had started on the fourth ropelength - solo. However much one might be irritated by Thomas' egoistic behaviour you had to take off your hat to his climbing spirit. Few if any, could have done what he was doing now. Solo climbing meant a greater risk of falling and zero support from a fellow climber. And Thomas was climbing at an extremely high technical standard - alone. We wished him luck over the radio and hoped with all our hearts that he and Trond would reach the top. They thoroughly deserved it.

ROBERT CASPERSEN

Robert getting ready for the evening stint. On the same evening as we reached the chimney, he fixed another ropelength upwards.

The Chambermaid

Next morning Robert first jumared up with my rucksack. He then descended to help me over the bergschrund with the big haulbag (I had drawn the short straw.) With what felt like half a carcass of beef on my back, every step was torture. I swore, spat and howled, but it was soon to get worse. Sixty minutes, and as many metres later, I started on the second ropelength. At every 20-30 metres the rope was secured to a running belay, partly to provide us with plenty of anchor points, partly to avoid too much elasticity in the rope, and most important of all, to prevent fraying on sharp edges. As I passed each belay, I pulled in as much slack as possible before clipping in the jumars on the far side. But with the next running belay far away to the right and only slack rope behind me, I found myself pendulating sideways. *How in God's name can I regain an even keel this blasted weight on my back? Better bring a baggage trolley next time. Only half-wits indulge in this kind of thing voluntarily.* When I finally attained the ledge it had taken me four hours to climb 250 metres. My one consolation was that Robert was struggling up behind me with a similar weight. As well as carrying his own rucksack, he was clearing up after us, collecting rope and protection. His total burden almost equalled my own 40 kilos by the time he reached the cleft.

Robert went up another 10 metres to strengthen the two copperheads with two stoppers and a friend, making a sturdy belay on which to hang our port-a-ledges one on top of the other. Deep inside the cleft we were safely out of the wind. The Russians' horror stories about full oil drums being blown several kilometres, had done little for our peace of mind. For the moment, however, there was a cloudless sky without a breath of wind, and Robert was busy with the next ropelength.

More to the right I reckon, Robert.' Sjur was prompting. 'Remember that little pinnacle we sighted? It's the only weak point on the whole upper wall and if we don't get to it we won't have a snowball's chance in hell.' At that point it seemed easiest to continue straight up, but Sjur was probably right and Robert abandoned the cleft, making for a horizontal ledge which disappeared round the corner. Before we started on the climb, Sjur had spent every spare minute scanning the wall: again and again, hour after hour. He never got tired of scrutinizing or discussing which was the best route to the top. While we were approaching the wall on our skis, he was forever asking questions like: 'Ivar, how high d'you think that vertical bit at the top is?' Or: 'I wonder whether it'll be ice or snow just under the summit?' At the time I hadn't given the line much attention, but it now became apparent how essential it was. Sjur, on the other hand, had really done his homework, memorizing every least formation. One kilometre of cracks, corners, overhangs, bare rock, pinnacles, snow and ice. Sjur was a true professional.

The sun seldom entered the cleft, and the temperature stayed at around minus 30 degrees, about the same as in a cold-storage depot. When Robert stood in the shade, tying his rock shoes he lost all feeling in his toes. But when he came out onto the bare rock he began sweating. Sun, or the lack of it, was the difference between life and death. On a calm day we could sunbathe stripped to the waist, but would have frozen to death if the very same place had been in the shade. There was hardly enough room in the cleft for two people to flap their arms at the same time. Sjur and I did not both need to belay Robert, and in any case there was no room for us both to flap our arms. Sjur crawled into the lower storey where we shared a mini-suite with balcony. Later, Robert was to have the top floor to himself. Both rooms boasted a panoramic view to the west, and in relation to Base Camp we were something like 250 storeys up. With floor and walls of thin nylon, and as much room to move around in as a child's lower bunk bed, it was as much as our lives were worth to unclip ourselves from the safety rope. In mountaineering, nearly all blunders have very serious consequences, and even though the terrain was not quite vertical, we had no illusions about surviving a slide into the bergschrund 500-600 metres below. Sjur asked me to check that the safety-rope hanging through the vent on the port-a-ledge was properly secured before he clipped himself out of the belay loop. With such a confusion of ropes, slings, and carabiners, it was vital to check what was secured where. If not, clipping out the wrong carabiner could result in an ice-axe, rucksack or even a companion plummeting to the bottom.

DELIGHTFUL GRADE SIX CLIMBING. EASY PROTECTION. I AM SOON FINISHED WITH THE ROPELENGTH. FEET STILL FROZEN BUT GETTING BETTER. Robert's voice echoed round the rock-face. Sjur and I grinned. We both had the same thought. If Robert could climb this part of the wall in rockshoes, we should be able to get the upper part done in one long day. With a little luck, we ought to be on Ulvetanna's summit in 2-3 days. Things promised well.

'Ulvetanna Base Camp to Ivar. Come in. Over.' It was Erik calling

Ivar here. Hearing you loud and clear. We're into the cleft and have hung up both port-a-ledges. Robert is leading one more ropelength before we pack it in for the evening. Any news of Trond and Thomas? Over.'

'Trond's called up already, you can hear his news later. I've been in contact with Lena at Novo earlier today. She says that three tractors are to leave Novo tomorrow. They plan to arrive in one or two days' time. To allow some margin for the boat, they hope to leave base camp on the evening of 4 February. Over.'

'The fourth is too early. It's the twenty-sixth today. That gives us eight days to complete this route, and little or no time for anything else afterwards. Tell them if it takes them two days to get here, then they ought only to need two days to get back. I assume Trond and Thomas also need more time. Can you hear me Trond? Over'

'Trond here. I hear you loud and clear. I'm a bit better and have been hauling and cleaning the route all day. Thomas finished the fourth ropelength solo. We are now hanging 200 metres above ground and will try to find a way upwards tomorrow. Over and out.'

'Ivar to Base Camp and Trond. It's so bloody cold up here, we're trying to turn the day around. If you don't hear from us by nine o'clock tomorrow morning, it's because we're waiting for better conditions. Over and out.'

'ON BELAY!' shouted Robert, marking the end of the day's grind. I took in the slack and secured the end of the rope, letting Robert rappel all the way down to the belay ledge. With Sjur inside the tent we had room to move around. 25 squat jumps, pause, 25 squat jumps, pause.

The sun almost never penetrated the cleft and the impression of living in a deep freeze settled over us from day one.

MIDGARD

I was breathing like a grampus, but it did not help much. Rope, belay slings and the limited space made it difficult to jump properly, but the very thought of freezing all through the night, kept me at it. 25 jumps, pause, 25 jumps, pause. Sjur was sitting inside the port-a-ledge in his sleeping-bag with all his clothes on, frozen stiff. I was still icy cold but had to make room for Robert who came down the rope - a graceful silhouette against the setting sun. For fear of losing my boots, I dared not take them off before I had both legs inside the port-a-ledge and the door zipped shut. The chances of being able to save your toes without your boots on were nil. To prevent them from falling out we hung both pairs from the roof. Together with various other bits of gear, this formed a vault with 48 sharp crampon points.

Each sitting in his own corner, we had the primus between us. Using benzine for fuel there was a real danger of explosion, but as Sjur put it: 'At least we won't freeze and we'll all go together when we go.' Every so often I opened the door zip, hacking loose ice clumps which we melted. Neither of the primuses worked very well, but after an hour, we had collected almost three litres of water.

'Bugger it! Ivar, you've knocked over the saucepan. It'll be lovely sleeping here tonight.' All I had done was, that in a moment of thoughtlessness, I shifted my backside, rocking the floor so that the saucepan toppled off the stove. In seconds, both sleeping-bags, and everything else within reach, were soaking wet.

With the exception of fire, this is about the worst thing that could have happened. Wet sleeping-bags and minus thirty degrees are a lethal combination. Our first opportunity to dry

A FANG IN THE JAWS OF THE WOLF

out would be nearly a day later when the sun reached the smooth rock. Until then, all we could do was huddle closer, something we would have done anyway in these cramped quarters. Ordinary nylon fabric with a hole at each corner and a safety rope through the roof ensured that the temperature was the same inside and out. With the exception of two pairs of gloves and some mittens, we had no extra clothing whatsoever. In a fit of bravado we had left our down trousers, fleece trousers and fleece jackets in the tent down on the shoulder. God, how we froze - our sleeping-bags froze - to the floor! But fall asleep we did, eventually. The last thing I thought about was something Thomas had told me on the boat, when I said how scared I was of sleeping in a port-a-ledge. 'Sleeping in a port-a-ledge is like sleeping on a kilometre-thick Li-lo. The view is fantastic. You'll love it, man.'

'I've never been so cold in a sleeping bag. I had to keep feeling behind my back, to make sure I wasn't frozen stiff. Bugger me, I'm glad that night's over.' Sjur and I crouched side by side, drawing on our damp stockings before struggling to get our wet feet into narrow inner boots. The night had been grim. I kept sliding in and out of a restless doze, too cold to sleep properly and too tired to stay awake. I looked forward to jumaring with a rucksack full of climbing tackle. Toil and moil, climb and stumble until at last the blessed warmth would course through my limbs again. My dream had become an hour on a jumar with a heavy sack. For the moment, it was delightful just struggling with my footwear. It was a battle to force the inside boots into the outer ones. I felt warmth returning from the exertion. Before opening the zip of the port-a-ledge, I made quite certain there was nothing inside which could fall out. Gingerly I propelled my hindquarters to the edge and stretched to get hold of the belay sling so that I could exit. The transition took my breath away. From lying cramped, but secure, in our little nylon box, I came straight out onto the balcony - two hundred and fifty floors up.

The weather was perfect. The mountains were bathed in glorious sunshine. It promised to be a wonderful day - if only we could get started before we were frozen stiff. But first, something to drink. After yesterday's fiasco I was taking no chances and rigged up a small kitchen on the edge of the balcony. The primus stove was still not working properly. It was ages before I had melted enough ice for two litres of water. The temperature seemed lower than yesterday, probably because I had had such a bad night. A drop of water soon sealed the crack in my eating bowl and by using cold water in the dried milk there was no danger of it leaking. Half my muesli froze before I could get it down, and I realized I was losing all sensation in my toes. It was time to get going.

Our chambermaid was dozing on the first floor. When we had gone he was to tidy up after the night's festivities. Our first section happened to be a traverse and once we had crossed, it meant that Robert would be able to use the static rope as a clothes line. Yesterday's spillage had frozen into ice which could be broken up and swept out when he emptied the port-a-ledge.

With a little luck, and sunshine most of the day, we could come home to dry sleeping bags and a tidy home. I was already looking forward to snuggling down in a dry sleeping bag and trying out a plan I had made for my down jacket - to stay warmer throughout the night. Robert had also had a bad night, even although he had been spared getting wet. Alone in a port-a-ledge with no one to huddle up to, it had been almost impossible for him to keep warm, however good his sleeping bag.

At long last we were on our way. Sjur was past the first belay, so I could start on the traverse. Nothing like jumaring to start the blood coursing through your veins. I was soon warm enough in my down jacket, but my feet were still icy cold. In time the extra warmth would spread to all parts of my body. Together with the blessed warmth, came the feeling of thankfulness - of just being here where we were; of literally having a bird's eye view; to have the privilege of penetrating a world for which mankind is not made, where life hung literally by a thread, or at least a single slender nylon rope. The first belay was a clumsy bit of work. Robert should have removed it on his way down. As things were, Sjur stumbled. 'Robert's an arsehole,' he grunted. 'Robert had best see to it himself to-morrow.' We had just reached the top of the rope, when the sun came out. First it touched on the back of my rucksack and then spread over my whole body. Forgotten was last night's nightmare. Sjur started to lead up a narrow ice gully. Had it not been for the constant stream of falling ice and small rocks, I would have dozed off in the heat of the sun. *Thomas and Trond, the lucky devils, are warm and cosy from seven in the morning until seven at night.* Today they had both overslept, not waking until nine o'clock. The air inside their port-a-ledge was so hot that they had to open the zip to keep cool, while at the same time we had been arguing as to who should stick out an arm for the radio. When I had managed to convince myself that I would survive with one arm outside the bag, Base Camp was already on the air, and we had to wait until 12 o'clock before we could make contact. The Russian ship was delayed and was not expected in Novo until February 12th. Nonetheless the tractors had left the base earlier this day and were expected to arrive the same evening. This sounded paradoxical, but the link with Novo was not too good, so Erik might have misunderstood. The latest news from Base Camp was that there had been an avalanche from the top of the glacier, and by leaning backwards I could see that the monstrous seracs overhanging the gallery had disappeared. Just as well Erik and I had not been there when it happened.

Sjur had to start traversing. If he continued climbing up the gully, he would be unable to reach the snowfield beneath the pinnacle at the base of the head-wall. The rock was flaky, and gave us cause for concern. There were no rock formations for the next 15 metres, so it would be some time before we struck a usable running belay. If Sjur fell he would come swinging back in the direction of the gully. When he had hauled up a load of bolts and long slings, it was just a matter of getting to work. It looked horrible, so Sjur took his time, looking for small irregularities where he could place a crampon point, before he edged himself further, afraid of rotating his leg and losing what little foothold he had. 'Watch it, Ivar, this is a dangerous job. If the last peg goes, then I'm in for a long, long trip.' The minutes ticked away. Half way up Sjur managed to hammer a bolt into a microscopic crack, clipping the extra rope in to a short sling. A couple of metres further up he yanked a little too hard on the rope and the peg pulled loose. *That one* at least would not have held a fall.

Having continually to move on the tips of his toes was gruelling work. Two hours later Sjur's legs were trembling like a sewing machine. Suddenly the hold under one of his boots

It was going to be a long way to the next proper running belay.

Sjur had to start traversing. The rock face was flaky and the next 15 metres were without formations.

loosened, but miraculously he remained upright, and after a few nerveracking movements, was able to ease himself on to a small ledge at the start of the snowfield. The remainder of the ropelength was much easier, and soon I was jumaring up. Fifteen metres below the belay, I could see why Sjur had asked me to examine the protection carefully. He had placed a nut-pick into a small hole. Around this he had tied a long sling with a carabiner. It was not exactly by the book, but definitely a creative solution which seemed as if it could hold a fall. A day or so later we were to discover that the nut-pick would not even bear our own body weight.

The next ropelength was easy, compared to the job Sjur had done earlier on. In some places the snow was loose and came away in huge slabs, but by and large, it provided good footholds, and before long Sjur had run out 80 metres of the 100 metre rope. After he had rigged up a proper belay in a crack at the foot of the pinnacle I started on the descent. Rappelling traverses is no more fun than jumaring them. Every time you have to pass a belay you have to clip a jumar onto the rope to take the weight of the figure of eight. In case one or more belay broke we had hitched all the ropes on to each other so that even on crumbling rock with uncertain belays the whole safety chain was pretty safe. The only real danger was if a rope broke on a sharp edge. In that case it would make no difference however many ropes or belay points we had. That was why it was so important to find belay points which reduced fraying, and to find time to hammer flat as many sharp edges as possible.

Robert would have made a perfect wife: redheaded, spirited and home-loving. Newly-made beds and dinner was on the table when the menfolk got home from work. Sjur arrived just after me and grinned all over his face when he saw how Robert had cleared up the mess. Our sleeping bags were virtually dry, 'freeze-dried' Robert said, when he had prised them loose from the port-a-ledge. Now they were bone dry after a spell in the hot sun. All we had to do was wriggle into them and eat our dinner. This was the life! On the other hand it had been a rotten day for Thomas and Trond. Robert had been talking to them a couple of hours before we returned. Trond was still running a fever and sat in the port-a-ledge all day, while Thomas had tried to find a way up from the grey hole, without success. There was no sign of the Russians, nor had Erik managed to make contact with them over the short wave radio link. Before settling down for the night I demonstrated a sleeping-bag with down jacket mattress à la Tollefsen. I zipped open the jacket, laying it lengthwise on the bag. Then I put one leg into the sleeve and wrapped the hood round the other, so that I now had down socks on both feet. The remaining sleeve I gathered into a pillow under my neck. Finally I pulled up the drawstrings, leaving only a tiny opening to breathe through. I woke up a couple of times in the night, congratulating myself on being almost warm.

A Temperamental Lady

Sjur deserved his first day off. So far, it was he who had built up the route, bringing us up to the head-wall. Today Robert and I were to lead. While we were skiing, we had noticed that the wall was concave, rather like an amphitheatre, and under the arched part there was a patch of snow. In the course of the day we would find out if we needed the port-a-ledges, or whether there was a shelf near the snow patch where we could pitch our little Helsport tent. By stretching the 100 metre rope up to the next belay we had enough rope to reach all the way to the top. Having established a routine, we were quicker in getting off, and at 11.30 had already started up the ropes. While still in my sleeping-bag, I had got the primus going early in the morning, and melted enough water for all three of us for the day. In our sleeping bags, we ate our muesli and packed our rucksacks. Fifteen minutes after crawling out of my bag, I clipped the jumar onto the rope and had scarcely time to become cold before I felt the blood coursing through my fingers and toes.

Two hours later Robert and I were dangling side by side at the base of the pinnacle, waiting for the sun. Robert was racking equipment and I was kicking at the ice to make more room for my feet. The first 8-10 metres looked 'do-able' to use one of Sjur's expressions, but the corner which ran under the roof, looked difficult; difficult to protect and difficult to climb. Robert laced up his rockshoes and changed to fingerless gloves as the first rays of the sun came sneaking round the corner. But even with the sun shining it would take hours for the rock-face to warm up. Until then, Robert had only a thin rubber sole and a woolly sock between his toes and a temperature of minus 30 degrees on the rock wall. The first section of the roof went easily and quickly, but when Robert had got past the overhang and into the chimney he went into the shade. It took him some time to climb high enough to be able to jab a large friend right into the chimney. With our biggest Big Bros as the next uncertain belay, the roof and the rest of the chimney turned into a nightmare. 'I can't manage this. Any minute now I'll fall, and then at I'll pull out the Big Bros and possibly the No.4 friend as well. This is the worst I've ever been through.'

My own experience had taught me that at moments like this the only thing that helps is praise and encouragement and more praise and encouragement. 'DON'T TURN BACK NOW. REMEMBER YOU'RE NORWAY'S BEST ROCK FACE CLIMBER. IMAGINE THIS IS HOME. EVEN IF THE BIG BROS AND THE FRIEND DO FALL OUT, YOU'RE NOT GOING TO FALL OFF THE MOUNTAIN! Perhaps this last was not quite true, but what Robert needed was help, not prophecies of doom. If having faith makes you think you can walk on the water, then it ought to be possible for Robert to fix a metre or two on the strength of a white lie. Not long after Robert, shouted back: 'OK, I'LL TRY CLIMBING OVER THE EDGE. PREPARE TO TAKE A FALL. *As if I'm not always ready to take a fall.* Seen from below it looked impossible, but on precipices and overhangs, Robert is a master of the impossible. Four or five ballet-like movements, and he was over the edge, standing with arms outstretched between the wall and the pinnacle. Without any more Big Bros's, he climbed the next 10-12 metres unprotected. But after the roof, the grade six climbing which followed was plain sailing. For Robert, at any rate.

I had the Devil's own job getting at the friend Robert had jammed deep into the chimney. Either I had broader shoulders, or else my rucksack was holding me back. Even after swinging out and swinging back again at full speed I was still a few centimetres short. I was about to give up, planning to get it on the way down when I would be without my sack (it was not my shoulders), but it was embarrassing not being able to retrieve what Robert had placed. By twisting my body into the crack and shoving the nut-pick in as far as I could, I finally managed to winkle it out. Twice more I found myself stuck, but after removing the Big Bros I was able to pendulum to the outer edge of the pinnacle. With a 20 kg rucksack it was a bit of a job getting past the overhang, but infinitely preferable to being stuck inside the chimney.

Halfway up the north-west wall we struck bad weather. Gusts of hurricane force swept the wall. Luckily, we were relatively protected inside the chimney.

I wondered whether I ought to lead the next ropelength in rockshoes. But the climbing seemed difficult, and I doubted whether I would manage in stiff climbing boots.

On the top of the pinnacle, I found Robert jumping up and down on a big snowdrift. While climbing, he had not noticed that his fingers and toes were completely numb, but now he was acutely aware of the fact. His fingers were soon all right, but his toes remained cold and without sensation. Now that there was no one below, I kicked away the snow to make room for Robert to change his boots. His toes were ghostly white. Even when I dug my fingernails in he could not feel a thing. There was nothing he could do, except change into dry socks and double climbing boots. His toenails were destined to turn black and fall off; but in the short time they had been frozen, it was unlikely that his toes had been permanently damaged.

I debated as to whether I should use rockshoes for the next ropelength. Judging by Robert's frostbitten feet, it would be stupid to use rockshoes, but the route looked problematic and I could not see myself getting to the top in stiff climbing boots. From the belay ledge I followed a vertical crack for 5-6 metres before the cliff inclined past the vertical. After jamming a nut securely into a bomb-proof placement at the top of the crack I continued to stem up a dihedral without further protection. When I rounded the top edge I was so far above the last piece of protection that a fall now would have gone straight into the belay ledge. Straining every nerve I scraped the snow out of the next crack, with no thought for ruined gloves or frostbitten fingers. At the second try I placed the right nut, breathing a sigh of relief as I clipped a short sling onto my harness. Idiotically enough, I was on the verge of finding myself in Robert's predicament.

The climb up to the snowfield looked fairly straightforward, but not the head-wall. Vertical, with occasional overhangs, it reared up 200 metres above our heads. The only possibility was to climb far inside the amphitheatre, where the sun only penetrated for a few hours at the end of the day. Neither Robert nor I would be able to lead in rockshoes in such extreme cold. It would be tantamount to cutting off our toes with pincers. Neither could we use the tent. The snow was as steep as a precipice, ending in blue ice at the base of the wall. Hacking out a platform here would take hours, and as like as not we would hit solid rock just under the surface. Ulvetanna began to seem like a proud old spinster who would not allow herself to be seduced without a stiff fight and long courtship. If she not been so beautiful and provocative, we would have given up long since. Before climbing the last 30 metres I had memorized as much as I could of my surroundings, as I knew Sjur would be cross-examining me all evening.

Robert's toes got frostbitten when he was leading the most difficult ropelength on the rock face. At the time, there was little he could do except put on double boots and keep on protecting me.

For the first time since coming here, we saw dark clouds to the west over Gessnertind and Jøkulkyrkja, and before we had reached the port-a-ledges, light flakes of snow had begun to fall. It boded ill for the transport stage on the morrow.

My fingers and toes were frozen, but not nearly as badly as Robert's. After fixing the rope in a horizontal crack off to the left of the snow, I rappelled, clearing the rope of protection. Altogether we had now fixed 280 metres of rope from the port-a-ledges and were ready to move camp the following day. With all the traverses and that heavy haulbag, there was not much to look forward to, and for the first time since we arrived here, I noticed heavy clouds in

Storm clouds on Ulvetanna.

With winds between storm and hurricane, it was impossible to move camp, so we stayed in our sleeping bags, counting how much food we had left and wondering what they were doing at home precisely then.

the west, over *Jøkulkyrkja* and Gessnertind. Before we joined Sjur down below, tiny light snowflakes were beginning to waft down. Things boded ill for tomorrow's transportation leg.

Saturday morning, and at home I would be frying a big breakfast of bacon and eggs. Afterwards I would take the children skiing. We would stop at Furubolmen (a ski lodge outside Oslo) for home-made buns and cocoa. Proper cocoa made with whole milk, not the watery concoction we have to drink.

The port-a-ledge is much warmer with a blanket of snow on it.

No long do I consider that nylon can tear or anchors, blow. I enjoy myself in my sleeping bag. Luckily, it will be hours before I have to go to the loo again. I am happy. Outside, the storm was raging, and the gusts rocked us pleasantly to and fro.

When we got back last night Sjur told us that Thomas and Trond had decided to turn.

Having spent yet another day trying to find a way up, Thomas had pronounced the route hopeless: 'It was just too fucking scary. A fall would have been fatal. I mean, you wouldn't have survived if you'd fallen on my last lead. It wasn't easy to leave the route, but I feel that I have spent more than my share of luck throughout the past 20 years of climbing - and only luck could have got me safe through the next fifty metres.'

That left only the alpine team. *If* we made it, then we would be first. But for the very first time there was an *if.* With wind forces between storm and hurricane, it was impossible to move camp today, and tomorrow was 30 January. It was only six days until the Russians would be leaving Base Camp. Not that it mattered. In any case, we were going to run out of food before that. Earlier today Robert had stretched out his hand and dragged the haulbag into the port-a-ledge. What remained were 17 packets of biscuits, 3 1/4 small packets of muesli, 8 dinner portions, 3 litres of soup, 13 packets of Knorr cuppa soup, 1 bag of chocolates, 1 bar of milk chocolate, 9 small bags of nuts, 1 small bag of cheese, 4 bags of dried fruit, 3 pieces of reindeer meat, 2 pieces of buffalo meat, 8 cloves of garlic, 1 1/2 litres U-nik sports drink and one home-

HAN SJUR.

made tart from Sjur's mother, was all the food we had left. It should have been more, but we had eaten well at first, never dreaming that the food would run out. Even if we rationed ourselves, the eight dinners would only last us three days. The biscuits and muesli might stretch to five. The other snacks were welcome, but did not add up to much when counting calories. Spread over five days it came to only 2,500 calories per man per day. Not very much. Our intake should ought to have been three times greater. If we ever got to the top, it would be by the 'slimmer-of-the-month' method.

Sjur was all for going back for more food, but for the first time I shouldered my responsibilities as leader - and refused. 'Before we can go down, we have to go back up and fetch the ropes. Even if we leave the port-a-ledges here, it'll take at least four days before we're back at the bottom of the head-wall. If we allow ourselves to be tempted to a rest day at Base Camp, or something else goes wrong, it'll take even longer. No, we stay here and continue when the weather permits. If we're not working, we don't need food. Not much, anyway. If each man eats 3 biscuits for breakfast, lunch and dinner, that still leaves fifteen packets. If we're still stuck here tomorrow, we'll drink tea. Tea isn't even on the list - so we can't say we've used anything up.'

Sjur was doubtful: 'Sounds all right, but what if we're here for a week? Or if we move up tomorrow, get to the top in three days' time and then have continuous bad weather and almost no food? Robert's not as fat as you, you know.'

'This storm's coming in from the sea,' I told him. 'According to the Russians, bad weather seldom penetrates this far inland, and when it does it usually blows itself out after a day or so. Besides I'm not all that worried about running out of food. If we have to wait for the weather, then we don't need to eat, and as soon as it clears up it'll only take us the best part of twenty-four hours to get back - without food if need be. I vote we push on as soon as the weather improves.' Sjur was not quite convinced, but seemed relieved that someone else had taken the decision. Robert was too far away to take part in the decision, and accepted the decision without demur.

As well as counting calories and guessing when the weather was going to break, we tried to work out the exact distance to the summit. I was the one to climb highest the day before and I estimated it to be about four ropelengths. Sjur reckoned six, and Robert eight. Our joint conclusion was that Sjur was probably nearest. Our reasoning ran on these lines: My altimeter had on average registered 100 m more than on the map. Lower down on the shoulder it had shown 2,500 m above sea level which corresponded to 2,400 m on the map, plus 20 vertical metres up to the bergschrund. According to the map, Ulvetanna's altitude was 2,931 metres above sea level, which put the vertical height of the climbing route at 510 metres. To where we were now we had used 220 metres of rope, which meant a vertical height of approximately 150 metres. As far as the upper belay we had used 260 metres, but because of the long traverse we had scarcely gained more than 120 metres in height. What remained was approximately 240 vertical metres or 6 ropelengths plus a little traversing. On average we could only manage two ropelengths a day, but on the last day this could possibly be stretched to four. Given one day for moving camp and two days to the summit and back, plus a day to get down, there would be food enough with a little to spare.

The wind rose in the course of the afternoon, giving the port-a-ledges a thorough shaking. With the tent fabric covered in rime there was as much snow inside as out. 'A real Fimbul winter,' declared Robert, referring to the cold period in Norse mythology of three years without summer. Each time anyone went to the loo, a mass of snow swept in. However little I ate or drank, I still had to pee four times in the course of the day. Sjur only did so twice, but each time Robert wanted to pee, Sjur had to lean out and steady the port-a-ledge to prevent it tipping over. Whoever went out, it was always snow that came in. Robert thought it was slow torture spacing nine biscuits throughout the day. 'Why not eat them all at once and then forget about food for the rest of the day.' Sjur and I ate only two biscuits for breakfast, thinking it easier to go without if we had a little in reserve. In the evening there was still no news of the Russians. Trond and Thomas had rappelled all the way down the wall the same morning, arriving safely in Base Camp.

Like most women, Ulvetanna disliked losing her suitors. Fearing that we too were planning to desert her, next morning she displayed all her charms. The sun broke through, and before we had finished packing, she had removed all traces of her outburst the day before. The ropes

Have you remembered your pills?

were still covered in snow when we started to climb but with Sjur as snow plough and rope-shaker, we made good progress to the head-wall. At regular intervals, small snowslides swept past us, but this did not worry Sjur. 'We'll survive,' he grunted. On the other hand, whether the jumars would grip the rope or not was the great question. Clogged with snow and ice, they slid as often as they gripped. It was rather like moving carefully over fragile snow crust, apart from the fact that it was farther down to terra firma.

Robert jumared up to the foot of the pinnacle with the heavy haulbag. His own rucksack was still down below. One of us would have to fetch it, simultaneously cleaning the route. I was not all that keen either on another trip or cleaning the traverses, and just stood waiting for Robert to volunteer. Admittedly, I would jumar a top rope, but as I removed the belays behind me, I would either have to negotiate the traverse in the same way as he who had led, or let myself fall in a long pendulum before continuing to climb. Almost every day, one or more of the anchors blown, and the distance between those which withstood the strain grew greater and greater. Earlier on Sjur's nut-pick broke loose when I was pulling at the sling in order to keep my balance. Whoever cleaned the traverse was going to risk some very bad falls.

Robert volunteered, taking it all in his stride, without a single fall. - as only Robert can. Sjur doubled up on the fourth ropelength and I on the fifth. The best place to hang the port-a-ledges was above the ice on the upper side of the snow-field. Sjur stretched out a single ropelength across the snow

Sjur making a bee-line for our new hanging camp site at the base of the head-wall.

Before we had finished packing, the weather lifted, and soon all signs of yesterday's storms were gone.

As we climbed higher we found many of the ropes buried under the loose snow. But would the jumars get a proper grip?

Robert cleared the long, steep traverses without a single fall.

At 0430 hrs our new home was bolted to the base of the headwall, and we were able to creep inside for yet another cold night's sleep.

Only a few metres to the next camp

There was still a whole Eiffel Tower left to the summit.

making a belay in the right hand side of the amphitheatre. While Sjur was hacking out a fifty centimetre deep shelf on top of the ice, Robert and I fetched our rucksacks and cleaned the remaining ropelength. Robert was ready with the video camera as Sjur and I were rigging the port-a-ledges. The last time we had assembled them, one of the port-a-ledges collapsed, wrapping itself round Sjur, who was left lying like an arm in a sling. His body-weight tightened the nylon so that he could not free his arms. Robert and I were laughing so much, we were on the point of falling over the edge, but unfortunately there was no repeat performance. At 0430 hours our new home was bolted securely to the base of the head-wall. We prepared ourselves for yet another cold night's sleep. And there was still nearly a whole Eiffel Tower before the summit.

The incline was too steep for us to pitch our tent, and there was steel-hard ice under the snow.

HOLTEDAHLFJELLA

A Hole in the Tooth

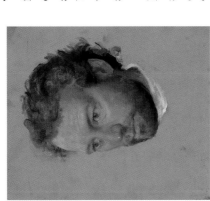

IVAR ERIK TOLLEFSEN

That night was the coldest so far. Sjur and Robert woke with fingers and toes that had lost all feeling. Even after an hour with his feet on my chest, Sjur's were still frozen. There was no doubt that both Sjur and Robert had frostbite. At the very least, they would lose their toenails, and have numb toes for some months. That was a price worth paying, but no more. Not even Ulvetanna was worth a little toe. The problem over the next couple of days would be to know where the limit went. This would become even harder when we climbed high above the port-a-ledges.

Although it was my day off, I still had to melt snow on the balcony. One of the primuses had given up the ghost and the other only worked if *I* held it by the leg and talked to it. In addition, Sjur no longer praised Robert's prowess as scullion. 'The water in my thermos was only piss-tepid. You can't make tea or anything else with that muck. I mean what I say, Robert. This is a complaint you'll have to take seriously.' Unless Sjur had his hot drink in the morning, and time to go to the loo, he was not himself. Robert was only 22, and drank what he was given. Previously, I had been unable to count how often *be* went to the loo, but here, where cooking and relieving oneself were confined to the same half metre, I reckoned he was worse than Sjur. I had not been to the loo myself for four days, and was now patiently waiting for the others to start off, so that *I* could enjoy myself with my backside over the precipice. In warm and glorious sunshine, it could be a rare and gratifying experience.

We had been discussing the possibility of reaching the summit this very day, but ended up settling for two more ropelengths. The weather seemed stable, and we had enough food left for three more days, so there was no point in risking the success we had within our grasp by a foolhardy dash for the summit. While Robert started on the first ropelength, Sjur stood shivering at the bottom of the dihedral. 'Ivar, I can't stand much more of this. My feet are so cold, it's killing' me.' We both knew that warming up would take too much time. It was imperative for Sjur to begin jumaring. The inside of the port-a-ledge looked like a deep-freeze with a broken defrosting system. To keep warm I borrowed Sjur's sleeping bag, putting my own inside it. When I woke up the sun was shining on the tent fabric. In the course of a few minutes I went from an ice-cold hell to a heavenly paradise without so much as a glimpse of St. Peter. From minus 30 degrees to plus 30 degrees. I sat in the door opening, two sleeping-bags behind me and bare legs dangling over the abyss. For the first time for many a day, I was warm right through to my bones. There was not a breath of wind.

I'm evolving into a climber: I feel safe up here in my little nylon box one kilometre above ground level. I've started thinking like Robert and Sjur: I used to be scared of vertical or over-hanging rock, never daring to look down. My worst nightmares were hanging belays or spending the night in a port-a-ledge. Sharp edges, loose stones or avalanche danger did not mean so much. It turns out I've been scared of the wrong things. Hanging bivouacs are safe. A dangling rope will hold at least two cars, and even a small nut in a good crack will take the same weight. If the nylon sheet tore I would still be banging in the safety rope. Now I can rely on myself, on our equipment and on Robert and Sjur. I dozed off in the sun.

BANG! I woke with a start, as a big stone knocked Robert's port-a-ledge a metre and a half sideways. So much for relying on Robert and Sjur and their protection. I spent the next four hours sitting shuddering against the back wall with my helmet on my head and two sleeping bags over me. Now and then I peeped out, and realized why port-a-ledges have sloping sides. It is to let stones and ice slide off instead of going straight through the fabric. Trying to drop off to sleep again, it occurred to me that my freezer had become something be-tween a baker's oven and a battlefield trench. BANG! BANG! BANG!

Two sleeping bags behind me and bare legs dangling over the abyss in the sunshine. For the first time for ages I felt warm right through.

Last night was the coldest yet. Despite an hour spent with his feet on my chest, Sjur could not get warm.

A new, steep working day.

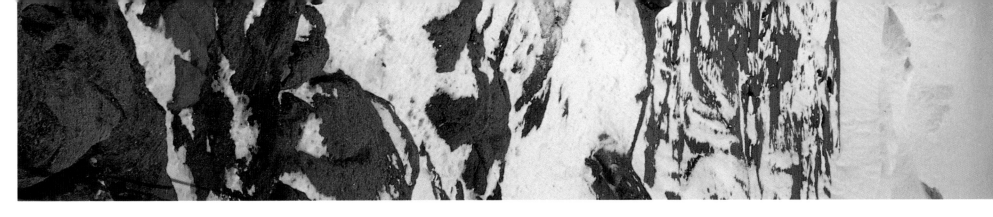

'Ulvetanna Base Camp to Wolf Cubs. Over.' I recognized Trond's voice on the air.

'Ivar here. We've moved camp, but are not on the way to the summit. I expect Robert and Sjur to fix 2-3 ropelengths before nightfall. How are things down there? Over'

'The good news is that the Russians expect to arrive here at 1800 hrs. Yesterday they fell into a crevasse and wanted to turn back, but Erik persuaded them to continue. The bad news came from Novo this morning. Storms are building up along the coast and are expected to reach us within 24-48 hrs. Winds of 30 metres per second predicted. *They should never have let us needed. A blizzard on the way to the top.* Over'

'Thanks a lot. As exposed as we are hanging, we'll be in big trouble if the wind gets up. Over.' I was not inclined to hear any more and was about to switch off, when Trond continued:

'Thomas and I were watching you from Fenristunga. You're almost there. Hang on, I'll get Thomas to tell you what it looks like from here.' The radio crackled and buzzed before Thomas's voice broke through:

'Hi, Ivar, you guys look very close today. It looks very good, yeah, it looks *very* good. We'll keep a close eye on you when we are up on Fenristunga tomorrow. Over and out.'

'Thanks a lot. Over and out.' It was just as well I had not switched off. Thomas' encouraging words had warmed my heart. 'I'm sure you guys gonna make it.' *That was good to hear.*

For the last hour, things had been quiet. The bombardment had ceased. The sun was still shining but with less intensity than before. Soon it would vanish round the corner, and we cold look forward to 16 more hours in the freezer. I was in the tent-door, facing south, my down jacket well buttoned-up and my sleeping bag wrapped around my legs. The landscape was awash with dramatic colour from the sinking sun. *Soon we'll have been here a whole month. I've stopped longing for home. Since we lost telephone communication, the distance seems so much greater. Perhaps those at home feel the same way too? Tomorrow I'll be ready for the summit. Freshly darned gloves and dry clothing. Hungry; but rested. - This must be the most beautiful place on earth. Everything so pure and so cold. No vegetation and no smells. Rock, ice, snow and sky. White, brown, black and blue. The red and yellow shadows cast by the sun's rays belong to a different world. This evening we polish off our last dinner. After that it'll just be biscuits and chocolate. The ice-slopes beneath me disappear suddenly into thin air - one kilometre above Fenristunga. Are those Thomas's ski-tracks I can see down there?*

'Did we hit you? I was certain only the aluminium frame would be left, but Robert said that weeds aren't removed so easily. He was right. Here you are, safe and sound,' said Sjur. 'We didn't mean it,' he added. *What did they not mean? That I should be sitting here safe and sound - or that they had not meant to kick all those stones?* Before I had time to ask, Sjur went on:

'This is becoming a bloody tough route. I led *one* ropelength and Robert led *two*, but there's still at least two rock pitches left before we get to the snow.' The day's work had been steep and arduous, with aid climbing through an overhang at the end of the second ropelength. The third ropelength had been a simple traverse to the right, to approach the line Sjur believed we must follow to the top. The feeling had come back in his toes when he was leading, only to go again on the stance. Day by day Sjur's and Robert's toes were getting worse. We could not remain here much longer.

When I told them of my conversation with Base Camp, they were both delighted to hear how positive Thomas had been. Oddly enough, neither of them reacted adversely to the threat of bad weather. We had come too far to turn.

'Now then, Nesheim, are we going to get to the top today?'

'Not got much choice, have we? We'll just have to forget how long it'll take. Obviously I don't want to stay up here. Not with that weather report we've got. Luckily the granite's looking better today, but we've wandered off too far to the left. In relation to the line we've decided on, we've reached a part where I remember there were some blank sections - where there was little continuity. We've got to traverse a little more to the right.' 'I'm dreading the descent.'

'Me too. It's going to take a whole bloody day. I try consciously not to think of going down when I'm on the way up. I'm planning it all right, of course I am, but just now I'm preparing myself mentally for what's happening here and now. Which is getting to the top. And then letting the next day take care of itself. Not to say I'm not looking forward to getting down again, of course I am. But I don't think you ought to do so, because I don't think you can concentrate properly if you do. I believe that...you shouldn't think about it too much. But that's just *my* way. I try to concentrate on where I am now. I take care to enjoy myself and not let myself dread anything.'

'How big d'you think the summit is?'

'NOTHING. Just a knife-edge of snow, a needle pointing to the sky.'

'Gessnertind is a much easier summit than this, isn't it?'

'You're telling me. That's a Sunday outing.'

'What about the north wall of the Eiger, then?'

'Well you don't take any longer with that than we are doing here. I think that *we* have more difficult ropelengths here. Maybe this isn't as dangerous as the Eiger, but I'm beginning to be uncertain of how dangerous it is here. You never know, if the weather breaks, that is. That would land us properly in the shit.'

'IVAR, ARE THERE ANY OF THOSE 17 WIPES LEFT FROM YESTERDAY?' Robert called from the balcony. Clearly he had gone to the loo without knowing if there was any more toilet paper, but a man's got to do, what a man's got to do. Each had his own way of coping. I still had three days to go. *Strange, Spur doesn't seem to have gone to the loo yet.*

'STONES!' My helmet already on, I grabbed the sleeping-bags, throwing myself against the back wall. The seconds ticked by - nothing happened.

'GET THE HELL OUT OF THE PORT-A-LEDGE. THIS ROCK CAN KILL A MAN!' I had not the slightest idea what the boys were doing but quickly gathered boots and jacket. My rucksack was already packed, and heavy. The jumars greedily gripped the rope. *What the bell's going on? What happened to the boulder?* My rucksack through me off balance, and I was constantly leaning backwards.

'WHAT THE HELL ARE YOU PLAYING AT?'

'HURRY UP, A HUGE BOULDER'S COME LOOSE A HUNDRED METRES ABOVE YOUR HEAD!' I already had cramp in my upper arms, but fear drove me on. 30 metres. 40 metres - *I'll never make it - but I've got to* - 50 metres - *only a little bit left.* 'STONES!' Fear hit me like a clenched fist. I bent my body forwards, my head between my shoulders. *Now!* Again nothing happened - just the sound of a few pebbles that whisked past. *False alarm.* 'GODDAMMIT, BOYS, YOU'RE SCARING ME OUT OF MY WITS.'

Well aware that the big boulder was still waiting, I hurled myself on to the jumars again. 55 metres - 60 metres. *What the hell, there's a piece of protection underneath the roof. A blasted peg that has to be knocked out. No question of my starting on that now. It'll have to stay there.* As I unclipped the carabiner, I swung out to the right and was left suspended in mid air a meter from the wall. 'IVAR, YOU'VE GOT TO BRING THE PEG WITH YOU. WE HAVE ALMOST NONE LEFT.' *This was all I needed.* Panic-stricken, I began to pendulum to get hold of the peg again. Above my head the rope was chafing over great sharp quartz crystals. Each oscillation brought a little shower of nylon fragments. Angst threatened to get the upper hand. I was on the verge of tears. *How many more times before the whole affair blows? Why is my life hanging by a thin 8.5 mm rope? Why am I not having any backup?* At last - I got hold of the peg and clipped in a sling. My hammer was behind my back under my rucksack, but finally I had it in my hand. Without caring whether I broke the carabiner, I hammered away. At the fifth stroke, the peg

ULVETANNA FROM THE SOUTH

IVAR, ARE THERE ANY OF THOSE SEVENTEEN WIPES LEFT THAT YOU HAD YESTERDAY?

While we were on the way to the top, Vebjørn stood down on Fenristunga and painted

With so little sun reaching the wall, you had to take pictures fast, while you could still wear thin gloves.

loosened, and sent me out in another pendulum and a fresh shower of nylon fragments. *If I don't turn upside down now, perhaps I'll manage. If the boulder stays put a little while longer, I'll manage too, and if the rope doesn't break, then I will definitely manage.* Over the last few metres up to the edge, I smelt an unbelievable stench of shit.

'Watch out when you reach the edge, Ivar. I forgot to crap before we started. If you just clip in here, I'll smear the shit on the boulder before we tip it over. In that way, we won't get shit along the whole route.'

'WHY THE DEVIL ARE WE FORCED TO JUMAR ON AN 8,5 MM ROPE, THROUGH AN OVERHANG WITH SHARP EDGES AND A PENDULUM INTO THE BARGAIN. AND WHY ARE YOU SO BLOODY WELL CONCERNED WITH YOUR OWN SHIT WHEN YOU CAN SEE I'M ABOUT TO DIE?' I was angry and frightened, but did not expect an answer. The boulder had worked its way loose when Robert had reached the belay and, after having left the job of protection to Sjur, had continued further. With Sjur's shit on top, we tipped the boulder over the edge, watching with some concern as it passed on its way within one metre of one of the port-a-ledges.

'That was a near thing,' said Sjur. *What was it near to? - that the rope broke - that the rock hit me on the head - or that the rock hit the port-a-ledge? If it is true that adrenalin is needed for success, then I have had a good start.*

The west part of Fenriskjeften taken from the north-west wall.

'HELL AND DAMNATION ROBERT, now the bloody Northerner has taken more than five hours to do one ropelength.' Less than 10 metres an hour - a snail would have had time to wave as it passed, except that up here there was no sign of life. Sjur was doing his best, no doubt about that, but the rope was not moving. The climbing was difficult. It was fourteen hours since we had left the safe existence of our sleeping bags. It was now three in the morning; the sinking midnight sun had vanished round the corner, and once more we were climbing in the shade. Luckily our belay was not completely hanging. After an hour's work, I had managed to hack out a little shelf 10 cm. wide at the top of the almost vertical ice slope, where Robert and I could move about a little to keep warm. It was incredible that we had managed in thirty degrees of frost, slight breeze, no sun and five hours' hanging in a climbing harness. Robert was afraid of more frostbite, and did all he could to keep warm - but the opportunity is limited when one is hanging on a rope.

If I get home by 20 February, I will go with the children on their winter holiday. I'm free- zing. A skiing holiday holds no charms. A Mediterranean holiday sounds better; imagine lying naked in the sun, slowly toasting; baking hot all over my body: fingers, toes, legs, nose - warm and dry everywhere; telling fairy-tales to the children in my arms. It is a dream to console one- self with. I am the only one to have escaped frostbite; eight hundred knees full bend' today so far. My old gym teacher would never have approved of them. Dangling in a harness without proper room for your legs, the knee-bends were bad, generating little warmth. At 30 degrees below zero, night and wind were horribly cold.

I was stupid to listen to Robert and Sjur who said we should leave our down trousers in the tent on the shoulder. The theory was that if anyone became seriously cold, we could go back to the port-a-ledges, warm sleeping bags and our primus stove. The theory was wrong. It is almost impossible to gauge the limits of endurance. The limit is different for each man. Cold comes sneaking up on you; toes feel a little cold and sore, but soon one loses feeling, and then every- thing is all right again: Wrong, it is not allright. Something serious is happening to your body; body fluids freeze, the walls of your arteries are punctured, blood plasma leaks out into your

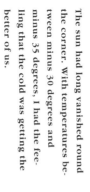

A hundred metres from the summit, we spent a long time aid climbing an overhanging crack

The sun had long vanished round the corner. With temperatures between minus 30 degrees and minus 35 degrees, I had the feeling that the cold was getting the better of us.

tissues. The dream of standing on the top of Ulvetanna with the Norwegian flag raised high above our heads, can quickly turn into another scenario: THREE NORWEGIAN MOUNTAINEERS TURN BACK JUST BEFORE THE SUMMIT. SERIOUS FROSTBITE. SEVERAL FINGERS AND TOES LOST. LUCKY TO SURVIVE.

The distance between success and tragedy lessened by the hour. We knew now that we had the summit within reach, and that probably we would arrive in the course of the next 20 hours, but I felt that it was many hours since we had coped with the cold. When I reached Sjur at the belay, he was desperate, screaming and swearing over why I had my own rucksack instead of his. He had no feeling at all in his fingers, and needed extra mittens; he could not manage to rack his gear or pour himself a hot drink. I had to cosset him like a little child, see that he did not damage the ropes with his crampons, and then send him off again to lead. When one leads, one becomes warm, but Sjur could no longer keep up his warmth. Sjur was the coldest of us all; he the tough nut from up north. He found it difficult to accept this, and looked after himself badly. *Was Sjur embarrassed by being unable to stand less cold? Ought I to decide to turn back?*

Before I could think things through, Sjur was on his way up the rope, which was anchored 10 metres above our heads. Numb, lifeless fingers gripped snow-covered rope; blunted crampons scrabbled on steep, polished rock. 'JUMAR YOU STUPID IDIOT', I screamed. But Sjur continued in his own cold panic-stricken world. Five metres, seven metres, eight metres, soon he would be able to clip the lead rope on to the uppermost protection. SUDDENLY he fell! *Bloody idiot,* I thought as Sjur came tumbling down, to stop dead a metre above the belay. *We must go down. Sjur is no longer thinking clearly. He is a danger both to himself and the team.* He is dangerous to the team because Robert and I had left much of the leading - and therefore many of the decisions to Sjur. He has more experience than any of us - probably among the best in Norway on cold, vertical winter walls; nonetheless, he also has his limits.

The fall shocked Sjur back to the world of the living. *Luckily.* Quickly and professionally he clipped in the jumars and climbed the rope to the uppermost protection. A six or seven metre overhanging dihedral separated him from the edge of the snow higher up. For the second time today, the étriers had to be used. While Sjur was swearing and hammering away at the peg, Robert came up and clipped himself in by my side. 'GIVE IT ALL YOU'VE GOT, SJUR. USE EVERY OLD PEG AND SLING YOU FIND. TO HELL WITH ETHICS!' Robert was yelling playfully, as he coiled up the rope hanging free behind him, and put it on top of the bag.

'Did you manage to retrieve that nut?'

'Yes. It was easy.' Everything was easy for Robert. *I had left that nut in, not because I could not extract it, but because I was afraid the rope would break when I pendulumed out. I was afraid of another shower of nylon. Better that Robert should die than I. It was perhaps not conscious, but if I were to be honest with myself, that would have been the consequence.* 'Would you like some chocolate?' I felt it eased my bad conscience to give up some of my one third share. As usual, Robert smiled and thanked me. He had eaten up his own ration many hours before.

'How are your toes?'

'Not too good,' Robert answered. 'I have had no feeling in them all night. If we find a good belay, I will have to try and warm them on your chest. I tried to get him to join me in another round of knee-bending, but he just remained hanging and watched Sjur struggling to get over the edge. For once the rope ran out relatively quickly and after a few minutes we heard Sjur bellowing:

'ON BELAY! IS ROBERT DOWN THERE?'

'YES!'

'I NEED ANOTHER ROPE TO CONTINUE. I RECKON WE'VE REACHED THE SNOW AT LAST, BUT HELL HOW STEEP IT IS.'

I felt a twinge of envy as Robert set off. Even on the belay, Robert was preferred. *Why exactly? Doesn't he trust me? I thought of how late one night he had come into my cabin, when he was drunk, and said: Do you know what I'm afraid of, Ivar? I don't know you - I don't know how you measure up. I'm scared of jumaring when it's you that's fixed the rope.' But that was on the boat. Since then, on several occasions, he had boasted about how good I was at organizing belays and racking equipment. He realized that I had done my homework, that he could rely on me. So why did he still not trust me? Perhaps the answer was simply that Sjur himself was uncertain; that he was climbing at the limit of what he himself could stand, mentally, physically and technically; that to have Robert at the belay was the security of getting help if he needed. For Robert was cut out for a vertical life, and he had a certainty that belonged to a bird. He moved around the port-a-ledges like a ballet-dancer. His knowledge of rope, protection, rescue methods, and everything else that concerned climbing was inexhaustible. Steep terrain was never frightening; just airy; good views, beautiful scenery, and a pleasant life. That was the answer allright. Sjur feels secure with Robert's talent and youthful strength. I would have felt the same myself.*

'IVAR BRING YOUR CHOCOLATE AND COME UP HERE. THERE'S PLENTY OF ROOM.'

At long last things were starting to happen. The belay ledge *was* roomy. The biggest yet - and with plenty of snow. In the course of a few minutes, Robert and I had kicked out a square metre where we could do knee bends and flap our arms. It was *lovely* being able to stand on our own two feet instead of dangling in a climbing harness. It was *lovely* having soft snow under our crampons instead of hard rock. And even better; the rope was gliding smoothly and steadily through Robert's mittens. Every ten metres it stopped, before continuing at the same speed. It could not be far now.

The next belay was half-hanging, but *now* we saw the top of the ridge. It would soon be five o'clock and an hour to our next radio contact. Jan was planning to send a balloon up to film us on the summit. *I wonder if it would possible to send along three bars of milk chocolate?* The last ropelength had been the easiest of the lot. The snow was loose, but underneath the ice was good and firm. Crampons and axes gripped like limpets. Sjur had only had to place four icescrews during the whole ropelength, and now he was on his way upwards again at the same 'high ' speed. The ridge looked difficult, and it was important that we came up as close to the summit as possible. Sjur disappeared behind the rocks above us and almost immediately the rope stopped. Gently Robert tried to pay out a little more - to see whether Sjur would take it - but after a while had to take in the slack. How long was Adam in paradise?

What little warmth we had worked up, quickly vanished. *It was as if it had become a habit to freeze, to be cold, to stamp one's feet, to avoid thinking about the sun, which, at this very moment, was turning the Base Camp tent into a sauna. Lucky devils.*

'I THINK WE'LL HAVE TO FIND ANOTHER WAY. HERE IT ENDS RIGHT AT THE BLANK MOUNTAIN WALL!' Robert and I looked at each other, both thinking the same thing. *If this lady doesn't give up soon, we might as well give up too. A few more hours, and we'll have to turn before it's too late. Everything depends on what the ridge is like towards the top. Fifteen metres of polished rock is enough to keep the lady a virgin.*

Suddenly the rope began moving again. At first we thought that Sjur must be traversing to find a way up to the ridge, but as the rope went faster and faster, we could not understand what was happening. Thirty, forty, fifty metres, and the rope ran out. Sjur gave it a couple of tugs - then all was still. Half a minute later, there were may quick tugs on the rope, the signal for us to follow. Sjur must have found a belay, and judging by the speed of the rope, it must have been big. *A ballroom floor where we can get some warmth into Robert's feet, and do standing jumps till the sweat pours off us . . .* When Robert had anchored the rope in the first ice-screw, I removed the protection and jumared up after him. I caught a glimpse of Robert, thirty metres above my head - making straight for the blank mountain wall.

IVAR, YOU'RE NOT GOING TO BELIEVE THIS. HURRY! Robert shouted - and disappeared into the mountain.

Text box overlaid on photograph:

What a picture! I can't stop taking photographs even though I'm freezing. This panorama cost me too much to be left out. Damn and bla... I lost my mittens, these great woolly things are impossible. Click; the last ... the film. One exposure isn't nearly enough, but I can't take my mittens off to chan... the film. Use your mouth. Hold the camera in both hands and flip out the spoo... with your teeth. Ow! the spo... is sticking to my tongue. Three different exposures; click, click, click. Perhaps i... will not be a picture, but at any rate, only I was up her... to take it.

Just under the mountain wall it was still just as incomprehensible - Robert vanished without a trace, and no sign of a shelf or belay ledge. Beneath me hung the rope - sixty metres down, before the icefield stopped in empty space. In front of me a couple of metres of precipitous ice, before the rock face towered up vertically towards the sky.

A HOLE IN THE TOOTH. The virgin had been expecting us. The old Norse gods must have been extra vengeful when they despatched the Fenris Wolf to the eternal hunting grounds. The hole in the tooth must have been his punishment for biting Tyr's hand off. At the junction of ice and rock there was a hole all the way through Ulvetanna, and while I hauled myself ahead with the jumars, I saw Arnesteinen and the other nunataks north of Base Camp - and sunshine.

The shelf on the far side was like a football pitch, or at least a wrestling mat. Sjur and Robert came towards me in their stockinged feet, and we stood and hugged each other with tears in corners of our eyes.

'Have you been on the summit?' I asked.

'No, we have saved the last bit for you. We thought that you ought to lead the last few metres. Without you we'd never have been here. If that was the case, it was at all events mutual. Without Sjur and Robert I could never have climbed Ulvetanna. It felt wrong to be first on the summit. This was first and foremost Sjur's mountain, then Robert's, and last of all mine. *Nonetheless they've clearly decided that I am to go into the lead the last few metres. It's better to say thank you than to protest.* With a lump in my throat, I climbed the last few metres to the summit of Ulvetanna.

'Alpine team to Base Camp. Come in. Over.' Interference. Then:

'This is Jan at Ulvetanna Base Camp. How's it going up there?'

'WE'RE ON THE TOP. I REPEAT, WE'RE ON THE TOP!'

At five o'clock in the morning we climbed the last lap on steep snow to the summit of Ulvetanna.

A HOLE IN THE TOOTH!

The view from the very top, facing north toward Tungespissen.

'WE'RE ON THE TOP. I REPEAT, WE'RE ON THE TOP!'

Down Again and Still Alive!

'Down again, and still alive!' Robert was smiling from ear to ear while the snow was thickly falling. From the cairn on the summit down to the tent on the shoulder, there was an invisible trail of abandoned stances and rappel anchors. We had left our mark on Ulvetanna. The virgin had become a woman.

It was six in the morning and the bad weather had reached Fenriskjeften, but for us the weather was no longer a question of life and death. We were down and we were still alive. Behind us lay 48 hours of continual toil and little food. After spending three hours in glorious sunshine just under the summit, we had crawled back through the hole and started an endless succession of rappels. Worn out and hungry, it was not long before the cold once more gripped our bodies. Sjur rappelled first, rigging the next anchor while Robert and I waited and froze.

'It's incredible it can take over an hour to rig a rappel anchor.' Sjur's excessive caution was starting to get on my nerves.

'He's doing the best he can,' said Robert. He did not like criticizing anyone, and especially not Sjur.

It was only twenty minutes later that the rope was tugged hard, and I lowered myself backwards and straddling over the edge. Compared to the first rappel on steep snow, this was like jumping from an airplane. Butterflies in the stomach reached full pitch when I passed the overhang and lost support for my legs against the rock. Each time I spun round I saw our tent half a kilometre beneath me. Nervously I checked that my figure eight and carabiner were properly fastened. *Relax, you've done this hundreds of times before. Another 15 metres, and you'll make contact with the rock again.* Fifty metres lower down Sjur was hanging in a sling and working with protection for our third rappel anchor. Protection for Sjur and myself, that is, but not for Robert. With so many rappels we had only enough equipment to fix one, at most two anchor points for each rappel. In practice this meant that Sjur and I rappelled from one good anchor, while simultaneously we had at least one back-up. When Robert's turn came, he removed the back-up and rappelled from a single point. The theory was that if it had held Sjur and me, then it would also hold Robert. Many climbers have nonetheless lost their lives on the way down, and even although Robert volunteered for the worst job, he was ill at ease.

The third rappel had been even worse. There was an overhang at the start, with 7-8 metres' penduluming from the end of the rope to reach the belay ledge. When we tried to pull it through, the rope was jammed. Both Sjur and Robert threw themselves over the edge to try and pull it loose, to no avail. Sjur was impressive in his determination when he jumared up past the knot, loosened it, and then cut the rope he was hanging from and landed on a small snow ledge a metre lower down. Admittedly he was protected by rope from the belay ledge, but I would never have done it myself, not for all the heaters in the world. For the final rappel we had spliced the thin 100 metre rope to a 60 metre rope to get us to the port-a-ledges. The bonus was that we could rappel a long distance without a belay, while the problem was to pass the knot while hanging free with a heavy sack on one's back. While I coupled both the jumars above the splice to take the strain off the figure eight, the wind started rocking me back and forth. For the second time in less than a day I saw sharp quartz crystals gnawing into the rope-

Robert

Sjur

Ivar

When we crawled back through the hole in the tooth, we moved abruptly from warm sunshine to deep shade and minus 35 degrees. Exhilaration at reaching the top evaporated in two long days of little food and hair-raising rappels.

Down again and still alive!

Stormy weather caught up at 'the Wolf's Den', but with only a short way to our tent, it no longer mattered.

Falling snow complicated the fixing of rappels on the descent.

Behind us Ulvetanna vanished in thick driving snow. But the images of eleven days' climbing and rappelling lingered still in the retina.

The youngest man carrying the heaviest load: Robert with the haulbag, 40 kg, and his own rucksack, 20 kg.

sleeve some metres above me. But even with adrenalin pumping through my blood vessels, my eyelids continually drooped. *My God, I mustn't go to sleep now. I'll have to warn Robert. This rope won't stand any more of that punishment.*

But all had gone well. And now Robert was standing beside me winding in the rope, while the snow was pelting down, thicker and thicker by the minute. Behind us, Ulvetanna was lost to sight in low-lying clouds and driving snow. A few minutes more, and we were able to crawl into the tent and go to sleep. I tried to remember how long it was since we had eaten properly, but the past three days melted together. Little sleep, much cold and toil had erased all the details. Before I dropped off to sleep, I remembered what Robert had said to me when we were cleaning one of the belays after Sjur: *'Ivar, you're a pretty good climber for a man of your*

Good to have both feet on the ground and dump your rucksack without fear of its dropping over the edge. After coiling the ropes, we crawled into our tent and gobbled up four bags of crisps washed down with a drop of aquavit. Not exactly a banquet, but how we enjoyed it!

age.' Coming from Robert, this was heart-warming, but what exactly did he mean by my age?

"You don't mean we've to get up now?' Robert's voice sounded plaintive.

'To hell with that. Not me. Push off Ivar, and leave ordinary workmen in peace. This means mutiny now.' Sjur drew his sleeping bag more tightly round his head, and demonstratively turned his back. After four hours' sleep it was miserable having to get up, but the count-down to our departure from Queen Maud Land had begun. In two days time, at midnight on 6 February, the Russians were to leave Base Camp whether we were there or not. While we were climbing Ulvetanna, we had discussed the north pillar of Kinntanna as our next goal, but now it was occupied by Jan Åge, Thomas and Trond, who were fixing ropes for a summit attempt the next day or the day after.

Breaks were already appearing in the dense morning cloud, and before we had finished packing, the sun was peeping through from behind a cloud on the horizon. Ever since we had climbed Jøkulkyrkja, a stinking, freeze-dried, dinner fart had followed us like an incubus, but after three dinnerless days, for once in a while we enjoyed pure morning air. After being on a steep wall for almost a fortnight, the snow slopes down to Fenristunga were almost like the Great West Road. It was only when Robert sent down the haulbag and watched it career away like a runaway racing car, that we realized how steep the terrain really was. The worst was sure to happen - and it did. The haulbag bounded over the edge and was lost to sight. So while Sjur and I lazed in the sun reminiscing over the four bags of crisps we had shared after the climb, Robert went round Fenristunga to collect our haulbag.

Since Kinntanna was occupied, we decided to make an attempt on Holtanna's north summit (where Thomas and I had turned a few weeks earlier). Leaving the others down at Fenristunga, I continued on my own down to Base Camp. As well as fetching fresh food supplies (not dinner), I hoped to persuade Erik to join us on Holtanna. Having looked after us others for a month and a half he deserved to get away from Base Camp and have a climb. Down the pass between Hel and Stetind I carried my skis on my shoulders, and enjoyed going to the loo without the usual encouragement from jeering spectators. In the distance I could see the Russians' enormous tractors, and felt a bad conscience for having dragged them here in our wake. The excuse that everyone else in Antarctica used the same form of transport, gave me no peace of mind. We ought to have managed without them.

Over the last few metres to Base Camp, I was half hoping for a little reception, but even after I had parked my skis and flung my rucksack down, the only person I saw was Erik. He did not seem at all keen on Holtanna, but went into the tent to pack a rucksack with personal equipment *I'm really looking forward to telling Thomas, Trond and Jan Åge about Ulvetanna. No doubt they think we did a good job.*

'No way, if Robert is leading an 8- off width crack.' Thomas shook his head, unwilling to believe Robert's grading of the route's most difficult rock passage. 'Ask any good

The North Summit of Holtanna (2577 metres) is an impressive sight from the North West. We called the mountain Holsttind ('Holst's Peak') after the then Norwegian foreign minister, Johan Jørgen Holst, who died while we were in the Antarctic.

With two days until departure, we remained in a tent on Fenristunga. After being thrown together for 11 days, we still enjoyed each other's company.

climber who has climbed offwidths in Yosemite (or elsewhere) what grade they climb. No one will tell you more than 6+ unless they have climbed a lot of offwidth.' I could not offer an opinion; 8- was far beyond me. But inwardly I was disappointed and miserable. *Why does Thomas have to discuss grades? Why can't he say instead: 'Congratulations! You did a great job. Was this really so difficult? Unbelievable!* Subsequently, on several occasions, I was to hear Thomas's doubt over the route on Ulvetanna. 'Was it really so difficult? Was it necessary to take so many days?' But never once did I hear Sjur or Robert questioning Thomas's grading of Kinntanna, where he graded the most difficult ropelength to 7+. Why was it obvious that Thomas led 7+, while it was equally obvious that Robert did not lead 8-? After all, Robert climbed to grade nine, while Thomas was rated at least half a grade lower. Personally I didn't give a damn about the grading on either Ulvetanna or Kinntanna; both routes were difficult. They were probably the most difficult routes ever done in the Antarctic. As an expedition, we had swept the floor in spite of having to turn back on the north wall.

The ascent of the north summit of Holtanna was a worthy farewell to Antarctica, and for the second time we experienced a bird's eye view of Fenriskjeften. The only flaw in our pleasure was that Erik lost all feeling in his toes at the first belay, and had to return to the tent on Fenristunga. I was miserable, and heaped reproaches on myself. *This was to have been Erik's summit; a little gesture of thanks from all of us who had been free to climb. But instead of choosing a peak which suited Erik, once more I have chosen one which I most wanted.*

Driven by a desire to climb one more of Fenriskjeften's summits, Robert and I continued without Erik. While the Midnight Sun sank behind the South Pole, we alternated in leading six ropelengths on snow, ice and bare rock. Sjur, who only wanted to go to the loo, had fallen asleep in the tent and had barely managed to clip the jumars on before we pulled up the rope. The Alpine team was together again. On first starting out on Ulvetanna, we had had the advantage of not knowing each other very well. You do not squabble with strangers. Now we had the pleasure of strong ties, woven together by many days of toil and tension.

Autumn and winter were clearly on their way, and the past few nights the sun had dipped below the horizon for the first time. The mountains were at their most captivating during the transition between light and darkness. Even the tiniest numatak cast kilometre-long shadows and the ordinary tinted picture in blue, white and brown acquired beautiful shades of orange-yellow and blood-red. For a whole hour we sat with our backs to a massive boulder, and savoured the view. We enjoyed ourselves together

Instead of going back up Fenristunga we ski'd down to the Sigyn glacier, continuing north past Kinntanna. We were hoping to catch a glimpse of Thomas, Trond and Jan Åge on the way to the top, but the distance was too great, even with binoculars. Just south of Hel we emptied our rucksacks and walked on foot to Fenristunga to fetch the sledges and the tent. I had gone ahead of Robert and Sjur and was only 100

From the north summit of Holtanna, we had our last bird's eye view: Fenriskjeften with all its unnamed peaks and *Tungespissen* in the distance. Kinntanna almost obscures Ulvetanna and Arnesteinen in the far distance.

beautiful and seductive snow surface. Was this the Wolf who wished to announce how easily he could swallow a tiny human insect?

In the course of that afternoon and evening we broke camp and made ready to leave. For almost a month Ulvetanna Base Camp had been our home, and it was with a melancholy feeling that I wandered around picking up some small shreds of paper and used matches. Shortly thereafter, the boys came back from Kinntanna, and were received with congratulations and a welcoming drink. Taken as an expedition, we had achieved our goal by the ascent of Ulvetanna, but taken as a group of individualists it was today's ascent of Kinntanna which made us ready to leave Antarctica.

metres from the tent when suddenly I trod through the snow with one leg. I had been following my own ski tracks from when I had been down to fetch food, but the penetrative power of a ski boot was, of course, much greater than that of a long ski. I pulled my foot out carefully, and went backwards a few steps before making for the tent in a wide arc. Having filled my rucksack I followed my own tracks back again, but got a new shock, when I realized that it was hollow under me. A few cavernous steps more, and then I was on almost safe ground. Compared to Ulvetanna's frightening jumaring and rappelling this seemed child's play, but probably it was the other way about. On the Ulvetanna wall the dangers were visible and violent - here they were concealed beneath a

We had been in Antarctica a month and summer was coming to an end. Even at an altitude of 2,600 metres, the sun sank below the horizon for an hour or so in the middle of the night. In the magical twilight, the landscape was at its most bewitching.

Climbing was varied and diverting, with a mixture of snow, ice and rock. The only thing that reminded us of Ulvetanna was shade and cold.

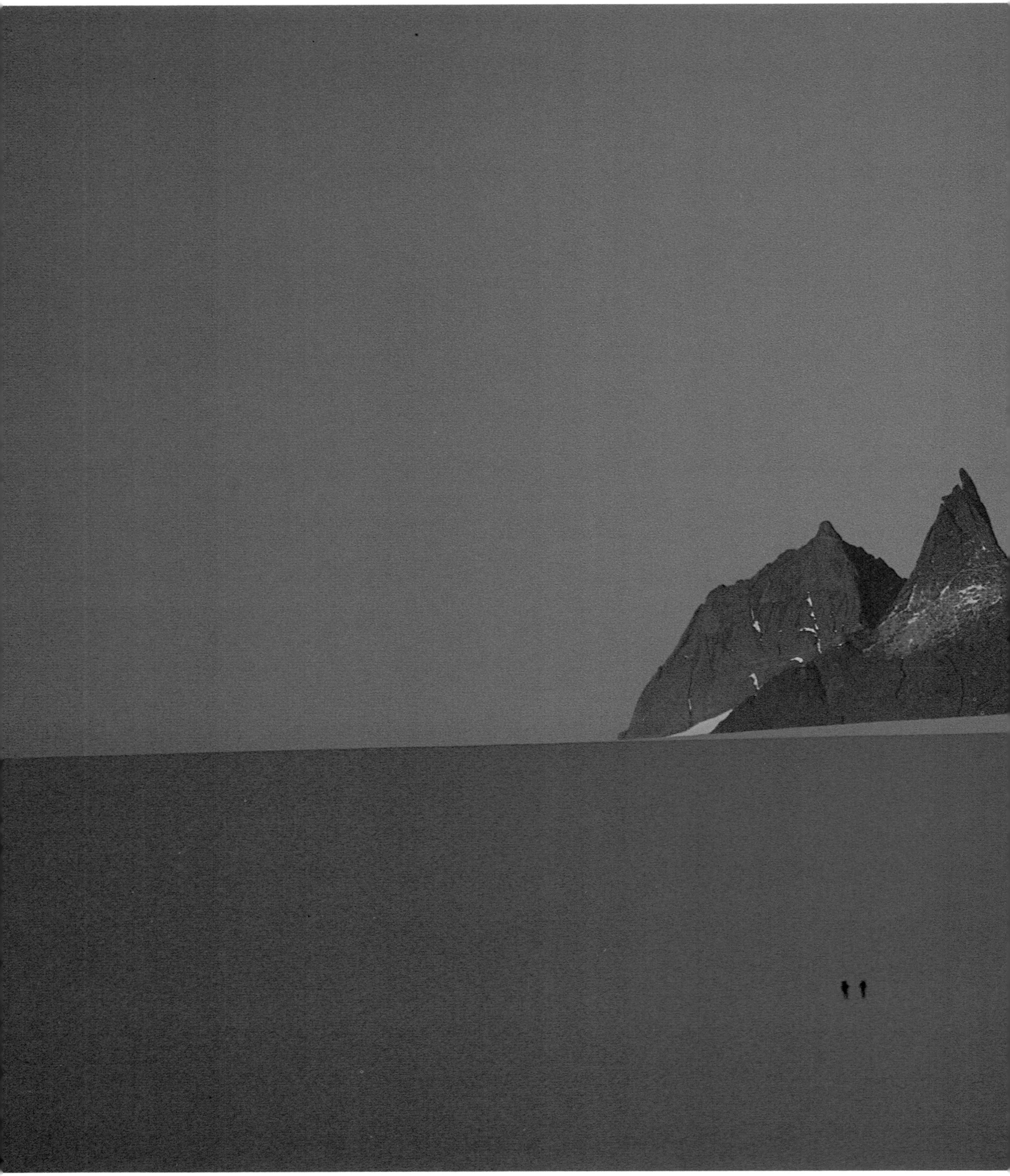

We left Ulvetanna at midnight, and set a course north east for Novo. Fortunately I had been sleeping before we set off, but woke up late the next day with a splitting headache. The transition from -30 degrees C and the purest air in the world to +40 degrees C and malodorous Russian cigarettes was horrible. I lay naked in a top bunk, ill at ease Thirty days of fantastic memories of Antarctica were about to be blown out of my head by a tractor which, despite its lethargic six kilometres per hour, had a noise level like a badly maintained jumbo jet during take off. That I managed to sleep at all, was due to the huge backlog of sleep piled up in the last fortnight. Suddenly it dawned on me. *I can escape. I'm a Norwegian - born with skis on my feet. Six kilometres an hour, unencumbered by a rucksack a piece of cake. Besides, the caterpillar tracks drop off at regular intervals, and that alone gives me a solid advantage.*

Shortly afterwards, I was down on the ice, heaving myself along to put as much distance as I could between myself and the tractors. Very soon I was joined by Jan Åge and soon we were alone and far ahead. Soundless now, the tractors were transformed into beautiful ghostly animals following obediently in our tracks. Antarctica was once again the close and beautiful. I looked forward to returning home to write this book, and experience the whole trip once more. I looked forward to showing the children what it was like in the land of dreams. Last year's hasty infatuation had given place to a deep and lasting love. *I shall return, I shall return . . .*

Homeward Bound

Thundering through the night at six kilometres an hour.

Bård, Jo and Odd had already been there a whole day when we reached Novo on the evening of 8 February. There was no hurry. The latest news was that the *Mikhail Somov*', the Russian ship, had a 15 metre long gash in her hull and was crawling at half speed up the coast. After Fenriskjeften and Ulvetanna Base Camp, Novo seemed hollow and dreary. Most of us longed to go back rather than we were longing for home. Before our departure on 17 February, there were various happenings to brighten the boredom; not exactly anything to write a book about, but it was fun nonetheless. Give a big hand to Erik 'Tank Driver' Nielsen, Trond 'Full Tank' Hilde and Robert 'Quick Draw' Caspersen.

Vebjørn Sand, standup comedian.

Annexed by Norway. . .

An artistic break.

We could do with a jalopy like this at home

Why use a jack when you can dig a hole?

Have the caterpillar treads gone again?

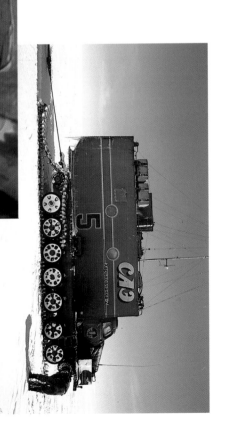

Forget about Robert and Sjur...

"Look at me. On top of a tank!"

Both the Russian base, Novo, and the Indian base, Maitree, lie on a moraine ridge about 90 km. from the ice shelf. Having heard rumours of gourmet food and female research workers, we invited ourselves to lunch with the Indians. It was nearly midnight before we finished our dessert, and just before leaving we exchanged gifts and postal cancellation stamps.

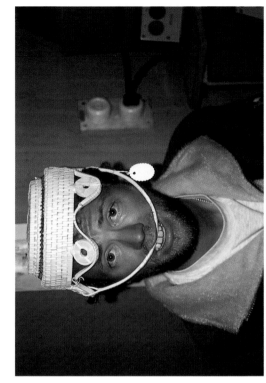

The Norwegian boss with the Indian gift.

The Indian boss with the Norwegian gift.

'Come on lads, it doesn't look like anybody owns this one.'

Full tank!

IVAR, WAKE UP! Jan sounded almost hysterical. 'Erik and Trond have stolen a tank - they're coming this way. Standing outside on the steps I heard the familiar roar of an engine, - and there it was. *I wonder what the Russian base commander will say?*

Where did you learn to fix the ignition in a Russian tank?

My dad should just see me now.'

Ready!

THE NOVO ICE SHELF 16. FEBRUARY 1994

Bård: 'There's the last of the aquavit'

Ivar: 'What about those two bottles of champagne David Durkan gave us?'

Bård: 'You can't divide two bottles of champagne between thirteen men. It's better to do without.'

Ivar: 'Who said anything about dividing? I for one have no scruples about organizing a small robbery, after certain other people burgled my private store a couple of weeks ago.'

Bård: 'The others'll smell a rat as soon as you start rummaging in the bags on the back of the truck.'

Ivar: 'But nobody will suspect our youngest. We can let Robert have a fifth if he wears his down jacket and smuggles the bottles out.'

Steady!

SKÅL!

All things come to him who waits. On sailing day we were ready at eight in the morning. They finally let us on board at six o'clock in the evening.

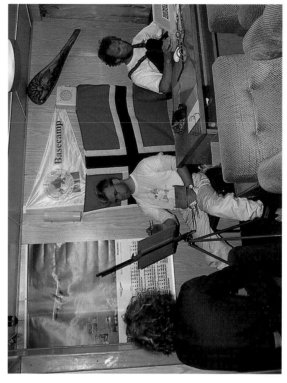

By day the Penguin Club was an artist's studio and an office.

With a newly welded gash in our hull, we chugged north on a course for Cape Town. Bad weather from the north-west reduced our speed from 14 to 3 knots and Jan insisted on holding lifeboat drill. On our way here a storm would have been an adventure, now it was only a delay. The *'Mikhail Somov'* was a tub compared to the *'Akademik Fedorov'* but the food was better and the crew a friendly lot. Having raided the Indian store, we reopened the Penguin Club, and on opening night all our regular guests turned up. Vebjørn made crêpes suzettes, Anita from Antarctica (Bård) did a striptease and Fat Banana and the Tank Drivers played nostalgic melodies from home.

'Good God, do I look that bad?'

ROBBIN

Who said anything about maintenance?

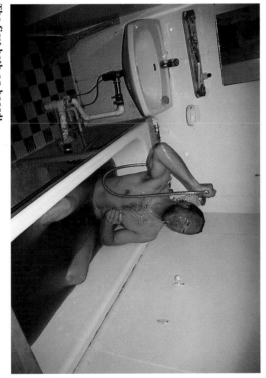

The first bath on board!

JÅGE

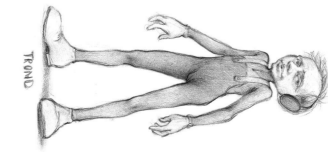

TROND

NILSEN

BY JO TOFTDAHL

The Skiing Party's Story

After climbing Jøkulkyrkja, it was strange to be sharing a tent with just Bård and Odd. Our intention was to follow the south side of the mountain range which runs from east to west at approximately 70 degrees south, going as far as the eastern extremity of the Wohlthat massif. We were then to make our way north, later north west, ending up at the Russian base at Novolazarevskaya, where we were to be reunited with the rest of the expedition.

On the way to their own camp, Erik, Sjur and Vebjørn dropped into our tent for soup and a tot of whisky. It was three o'clock in the morning, and our first dinner (we were having scallops) was almost ready. Henceforth we three would only have each other for company. We had been part of a boisterous gang of thirteen, with corresponding fuss and bother. Now we were only three. And, here we were, sitting quietly in our very own tent. I glanced at Bård who was sitting placidly in the middle. Bård had no special preferences as to where he wanted to spend the next thirty days and nights. Odd and I, on the other hand, are creatures of habit and had bagged places on the right and left hand side respectively. This was the first time I had been with Bård. With the exception of the few hectic weeks preceding our departure, I had scarcely known him. Truth to tell, I was a bit worried about the state of his health. His struggles with the sledge on the approach to Jøkulkyrkja had not exactly reassured me. His sunny temperament, however, won us over. When our ship lay waiting for the South Africans to discharge their cargo, Odd and I spent our time becoming accustomed with Antarctic ice and snow. Bård, on the other hand, chose to stay on board, hobnobbing with his new-found Russian friends.

I knew Odd's physical qualities: 'the world's fittest grandfather', and the first Norwegian on Mount Everest. Bård had called him the most experienced wheeler dealer in the whole of Norway. Odd and I had been on many a ski-tour together, besides which we occasionally worked together. So even if I did not know Bård, I certainly knew what Odd was capable of. If the truth be known, I was a little uncertain of my own form, feeling I had not enough time to train. Ivar had only given me three weeks' notice. I had discussed Queen Maud Land a year and a half ago, but unfortunately there was no place for me, until one of the climbers dropped out at the beginning of December. From then on life became one long, hectic round of meetings and discussions, mostly in my basement or Ivar's garage. There was little time for physical training.

When Bård, who has a well developed taste for the fleshpots of civilization, produced a can of deep frozen beer to celebrate the first scallops dinner. I sniffed at the idea of canned beer in the middle of the Antarctic, but there was no getting away from it - the stuff certainly went down well after a long and exhausting day. We slept - our mouths still full of half-chewed scallops.

Next morning we wondered who would be languishing at Base Camp - and who was to climb Gessnertind. Not that it made any difference, we wouldn't get to know until the expedition was over, as we had no means of getting in touch. Our only means of communication was our Argos transmitter. Programmed into this were six pre-arranged messages. No. 1 was: 'All's well', while no. 6 was: 'Need immediate help, bad landing conditions'. The messages were transmitted by satellite to Toulouse, then home to Oslo, from there to the Russian Polar Institute in St. Petersburg, and finally by radio to the Russian base at Novolazarevskaya in Queen Maud Land,

JO TOFTDAHL

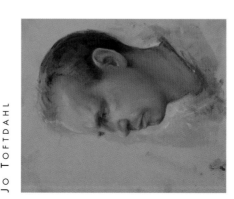

BÅRD STOKKAN

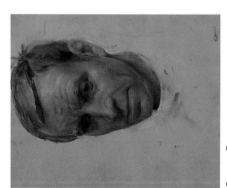

ODD ELIASSEN

Søkkhornet under a full moon.

where our Russian interpreter and liaison officer Lena, was waiting in readiness. After all this complexity I was beginning to fear that 'immediate help' had taken on a new significance.

Jan Haugland, of the Polar Institute in Norway, had advised us to keep as far to the south as possible. This way we hoped to avoid the crevassed areas formed where the ice flows down and is forced through the mountain range in narrow glaciers. All in all we were to travel about 550 kilometres. This is roughly the same distance as a crossing of the Greenland icecap. We had food for thirty days, and considered we had plenty of food and time. Starting out, our sledges weighed about 75 kg each, chock full and heavy enough. I did not envy the 'solo' travellers' their sledges, which were 50 kg heavier than ours. It must have a real struggle hauling a load of 125 kg. on the rough abrasive snow.

The worst part of the climb, up to 2,500 m, we had already covered on the way up to Jøkulkyrkja. So now we looked forward to enjoying ourselves for the rest of the journey. At the end of a long day's march southwards, we were still content when we made camp. The map however did not agree with the terrain. Our position by satellite must be misleading. We must have gone further than it indicated. We thought that this could be explained by a bad map and a remote satellite. It was not until next day, that we began to doubt our progress. The Djupedalshausane peaks were not getting any nearer and we had counted on arriving in the course of the morning. As it was, it turned out the navigation satellite was not as misleading as we had believed. What was true was that we were not going as quickly as we had expected. But why? Odd thought it was all the sastrugi. I blamed the abrasive snow, while Bård pointed out that the sledge was much too heavy. The following night we treated ourselves to 'two-mile-chicken' to celebrate the 20 kilometres we had covered that day. Our spirits began to droop. We would never finish those 550 kilometres.

On the approach to Jøkulkyrkja the sun had been so hot that we wore only our vests. There was scarcely a puff of wind until we reached the summit. But we soon noticed the difference when we left the mountains to continue south. In Queen Maud Land the prevailing wind blows from the south-east, 75% per cent of the time. We therefore had a head wind and,

On our very first day, Trollslottet ('The Trolls' Castle') gave us an idea of what to expect in the way of wild, fantastic scenery.

Luckily it's 24 hours to next time.

together with considerable frost, life was somewhat miserable. After only two days of this, my nose was badly frostbitten, resulting in a sore which I had to live with for a month. This was actually the worst cold injury on the whole journey. Our faces were swollen from wind and cold, but gradually that subsided. We took to calling Bård Al Capone. He had acquired those rounded, swollen cheekbones and greasy, slicked back hair. I had only to remove my mittens, and the cold was biting my fingers. If I lowered my hood in a sudden fit of optimism to the enjoy the view with a little wider angle of vision, my cheeks burned with the cold. In the long run it was frustrating, having to hide inside the hood of my anorak, which was covered in rime and weighed down with ice. As long as we kept on the move, we managed to keep warm, but on days when the wind was at its worst, we were frozen to the marrow - even on skis. Fumbling with tent poles, sledge harnesses and gas bottles was no joke. Once your hands got cold it was almost impossible to get them warm again. Mostly we managed, and at least we did not have to consider amputating limbs. Worst of all was going to the loo, when for obvious reasons, we had to do without mittens. We had different theories as to which was the best way to squat. Odd sat facing the stormy blast, with his bare backside sheltered from the wind. I preferred the wind on my back, with the drift snow blowing directly on my behind. As the one with the most active bowels, Odd had much more experience, so I ended up taking his advice and turned to face the wind as well.

We had been instructed to take all our refuse back with

us out of Antarctica, including urine and excrement. This posed gigantic problems. With all the melted snow we drank, we were going to end up with a rather heavier load than when we started. There was one loophole; it was permitted to pee on blue ice on its way to the ocean. We reckoned that all the ice in Antarctica ends up in the sea in the course of a few thousand years, so with an easy conscience we peed on the ice. All refuse that could not be burned, we took with us.

Owing to the cold we did not go in for long lunch breaks. We trudged steadily on, seldom stopping, nibbling chocolate on the way. Bård tended to lag behind. Usually we waited for him, but some days when the weather was bad he could go for a whole day without ever catching us up. It was far too cold to stop and wait. Odd and I each had our own daily routine, and generally we ski'd a hundred metres one behind the other. We took it in turns to lead, exchanging a few words when it was time to change over, or perhaps borrowing ski-wax from each other. The rest of the day we were alone. I resembled a hermit crab cocooned in a shell of frozen garments. At times the scenery was so fantastic I could have gazed at it all day long. Other days were just plain monotonous grind. We trudged on day after day, saw Glopeneshanen rise up on the horizon, only to disappear a few hours later. On such days I let my thoughts roam at will. Odd admitted to erotic fantasies. Vebjørn had proclaimed him Norway's most priapic man; had he not demonstrated his fatal attraction on board the 'Akedemika'? Galina, the waitress, always gave Odd double portions. She even went to his cabin with an invitation for coffee, but Odd hid behind the curtains. I also tried erotic daydreaming. It sounded a good way of making the time pass. I was not much good at it though. Imagination was soon dulled by the somewhat unerotic surroundings. I tried other thoughts to make time pass. If I could only succeed the leaden days would go so much faster.

With gusts up to hurricane force, we had to leave the tent up for most of the day.

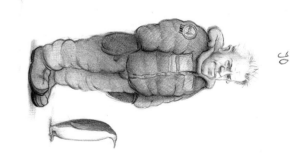

By and large it was the trivial everyday things which occupied my thoughts. I could debate for half an hour whether I ought to loosen the drawstring on my anorak hood - or I observed the ice piling up on my goggles. When it did, I considered how long it would take before Odd became invisible in the frozen condensation. Another thing to think about was how long it was since I had looked at my watch. Spinning out the time in small portions seemed a useful way of keeping it under control.

On the first leg of our journey, the hours dragged. The sledge was heavy, ditto the snow, and we were making little headway. It was hard work to which we were unaccustomed. Slowly things began to improve. Above all, I grew accustomed to this kind of existence, and found peace of mind. The days followed one upon the other, routines were established and everything fell into place. No longer did kilometres and hours dominate our thoughts. I ski'd along in a kind of daze, day-dreaming about everything under the sun. Often I thought of Maj Brit at home, and of the child waiting for us in Brazil. I might brood over whether I had remembered to arrange everything at home before I left, or look forward to all the nice things we were going to do when I got back.

We invariably put the tent up with the door facing north-west. Consequently, my usual place on the right hand side caught the warm afternoon sun. Odd, on the other hand soon started complaining about rime on the tent and frozen hands. In the mornings it was the other way about. Then the rime hung in great swathes above my head, while Odd warmed his hands on his side of the tent. Bård, being pig-in-the-middle, was satisfied all the time.

A couple of days after leaving Jøkulkyrkja we met our first crevasses. In all probability we had already crossed some concealed ones before it dawned on Odd that we were actually standing on a snow bridge. After that they followed thick and fast. We decided that one of us would have to go ahead in order to find a safe route, while the others followed precisely in his tracks. Hitherto, we had ambled along carelessly.

On board the 'Akademik Fedorov' we had studied photographs of part of the region, showing certain well-crevassed areas we were advised to avoid. We had dutifully marked these off on the map. Now it appeared that there were considerably more than had been visible on the aerial photographs. We altered course towards the south, hoping to escape the crevasses. However, that took us into a confusion of white ridges and hollows, instead of the great flat expanses for which we had hoped. Here there were crevasses, mostly concealed, as far as the eye could see. There was no point in turning south. After all, it had never had been our intention to head for the South Pole, which was all of 2,000 km away. The only alternative remaining, was to go ahead, threading our way through the crevasses.

On the boat from Cape Town we had heard of the fatal accident that had befallen Monica Kristensen's expedition in similar circumstances. This rather dampened our taste for taking risks. Would it be better if we were all roped together? I suggested it would be best using a rope to get through the most difficult areas. Odd answered that it would be wisest to give the worst patches a wide berth - a telling argument, we thought. At any rate, we realized it would be no joke being roped up when trying to haul a heavy sledge across huge sastrugi and wide crevasses. That settled, the rope stayed where it was - in the sledge. Most probably we would all have failed the Norwegian Glacier School's course, but we did get safely through in the end. Odd and I took turns at leading. It is a frightening experience going first over a snow-bridge; you hold your breath, make yourself as weightless as possible then head for the far side as fast as you possibly can. Nonetheless, the sledges broke through now and then.

The advantage of this kind of terrain was that it gave us more than enough to occupy our thoughts. The hours took care of themselves, even if the kilometres seemed even more interminable. Crossing 10-15 metre crevasses became almost a habit. We must have crossed hundreds of them, soon regarding ourselves as experts in reading the snow, to detect the chasms under the undulations, and gauging where it was safest to cross. One day, while we were walking, instead of skiing, because of the hard going, Odd broke through. I had crossed the same place, but must have gone a few centimetres to one side. Odd suddenly felt what it was like to hang by the arms above a deep blue, bottomless chasm. Luckily the snow held, and he was able to haul himself back up. Later on, we came across places where the snow seemed flat and even without the least hint of crevasses, but when you stuck in a ski stick, a huge patch might collapse. This gave us an excellent opportunity of studying the depths of these hidden chasms. Bård too had

an accident, when we were on our way to climb Altertavla (the Triptych). He trod through the surface with both feet, but managed to fling himself forward to safety. He broke his ski stick, but luckily escaped sliding down into the crevasse. Bård reckoned that was worth a broken ski stick.

The crevasses were partly the cause of our debating a change of route after eight or nine days. It had dawned on us that the route which we planned to take would lead us further into other crevassed terrain until we fetched up at the Wohlthat massif itself. All this time we'd had this fantastic mountains to the north. Odd, who likes nothing better than climbing mountains, became more and more frustrated:

'Look here, it's horrible to travel to the other end of the world, just to see these summits from miles away. Tomorrow we head for the mountains instead of threading our way through this Emmenthaler cheese.' Bård and I heartily agreed with him, even though Ivar's plan was for us to go all the way round the massif. It would be a shorter route, but we all three considered that mountain climbing was an interesting alternative. The only thing against it was that the 'real climbers' would think we were stealing their thunder if we ended up with more first ascents then they. We decided to chance it. Next morning we set off north for the mountains, turning our backs on Glopenesranen - the peak we had been staring at for the past few days, without it ever appearing to get any closer.

After a long day, we reached dry rock and our spirits rose. We had fixed routines for making camp, varied, of course, with the state of the weather. Whenever possible we dug the tent into the

snow, putting up a windbreak using the sledges. We hung up garments and bags to dry, lit the stove, and rigged radio antenna in the direction of East Africa. Odd had his own little short wave set, so we could listen in to the Norwegian radio's foreign service. Every evening at seven we crowded round Odd, holding our breath; had he found the right frequency? This was Odd's baby. Both Bård and I were keen to help, but Odd declined to let go of his receiver. Mostly we managed, even if sometimes we missed the beginning of a programme. Local reports often followed the main news. If it did not happen to be Finnmark, (his home county) Odd preferred to listen to the BBC news from Swaziland or Burundi. Bård and I were of the opinion that the news from our own home counties were more interesting. This discussion tended to repeat itself every evening, except when it was the Norwegian radio's foreign service request programme. Then there was happiness and unity. We drank toasts in refreshments we had brought with us, and conviviality reigned supreme.

The climate changed for the better when we reached the mountains. Here we were sheltered from the wind, which made it pleasant in the sun. We had our first proper lunch-break, sitting in the sun, airing our socks and drying our boots. It is a unique experience, sitting in the sun in only your singlet, being roasted on your stomach with twenty five degrees of frost on your back. A tiny puff of wind was enough to make us shiver with the cold.

It was better to be looking down than looking up.

It was quite another experience exploring the territory among mountains, ice falls and moraines. Our small caravan wound its way slowly forward.

One night we lay in Death Valley. Death Valley could have ended in tragedy. Odd got the name from a newspaper article at home about a fishing trip on Hardangervidda in the Norwegian mountains. I was about to light the burner to make our breakfast. We were using high octane fuel, which is not easy to see if it leaks onto the floor of the tent. But it burns beautifully. When I lit the stove, flames shot up - I thought the whole tent was on fire. Bård and Odd came diving to the rescue. Luckily, the damage was confined to holes in the tent floor and the inner lining. In addition, my beloved quiff was two inches shorter. Rather subdued, we spent the rest of morning inside the tent. I did not dare think of what would have happened had the tent burned down. It was far to human habitation.

We had already made one ascent. One of the southernmost peaks in the range, Müllerkammen, lay right in our path, so we climbed it one afternoon not long after we had started out. In our opinion there were far too many German names in the Norwegian sector, so we renamed it Loketind. We spent one night in a place resembling a family camping site at home in Norway - an ideal starting point for ascending two more peaks. The first we called Mount Jorun, after Bård's mother - it happened to be her birthday. The next day we were on Sandeggtind,

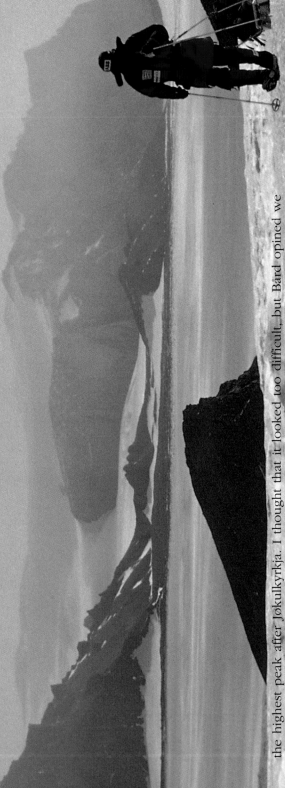

the highest peak after Jokulkyrkja. I thought that it looked too difficult, but Bård opined we would manage. Odd vacillated. We set off up a long, steep snow-covered incline. When the skiing gave out and climbing began, Odd went first. He discovered a good route which ended in a steep ridge. We followed this all the way to the top, and were rewarded with a view, the like of which few people could have seen: hundreds of needle-sharp pinnacles interlaced with the palest of blue ice-streams and with moraines which looked as though they had been painted on the ice - the whole fairy-tale panorama bathed in Antarctic sun in the crystal clear air.

Back in the tent, we celebrated our conquest with the rest of the aquavit, and hunted through the rations until we found a chicken casserole. We were becoming fed up with scallops. For the past week, our menu had been dominated by scallops, so that we began to fear malnutrition because of an unbalanced diet. Between the two alternatives, chicken casserole strengtehened with chicken soup was the clear favourite.

There were still a couple of peaks close by, but reluctantly we had to leave them - we still had quite a way to go. So now we left our family camping site, heading north west towards new and exciting, untouched terrain. The sastrugi were lower and more rounded, where the winds were not so strong. Further south the sastrugi had made life a misery. Sledges overturned, skis slipped backwards, and often we had the feeling of being torn off at the waist when the sledge got stuck in sastrugi. Bård constantly maintained that he had seen worse in Greenland, but the ones here could be over six feet high amd that was quite enough for me.

On the way out of 'Death Valley'

From the start of the journey, we had worked out strict routines for our tent life, and we concentrated on doing everything in the right way every single day. First we had tomato soup as soon as we had pitched the tent. The news followed, while our dinner, to which we added Russian chilli peppers and garlic, bubbled on the burner. After dinner, came a handful of crisps or peanuts, followed by sweet biscuits, which produced a raging heartburn. We were thirsty too, but the thought of having to get up and go out in the middle of the night, put us off drinking too much in the evenings. No one thought that it was particularly amusing to get up in the middle of the night in a rime-encrusted tent, and then to creep out in their underclothes, and then relieve themselves while the wind cut through to the marrow.

Mornings in the tent could be quite unpleasant. We always awoke to a fine shower of white rime from above our heads. Odd had the job of removing the rime. He did this by going outside and proceeding to treat the tent as if he were a boxer having a practice round or two. As a result, a layer of rime crystals settled on sleeping bags, clothes and tent floor. It was a trying job to sweep it out of the tent before we put the kettle on for breakfast, and our tempers may be said to have raised the temperature.

We climbed Gjeruldsenhøgda on a fine, sunny day. On our way up we actually found a stretch of sand which reminded us of a beach - the only thing missing was water. We lay there dreaming of more northerly latitudes. Later we passed some incredible formations in the mountain. We came across huge potholes and 'mushrooms' usually associated with river beds and

coastal cliffs eroded by water. Here, however, it was wind and snow that had done the work.

The next day we explored a long glacier arm between two rows of unnamed peaks. The wind made it hard going. Bård measured 27 metres per second on his anemometer. This is a full storm on the Beaufort scale. We began searching for a place out of the wind for our tent - if the tent blew down it would be difficult pitching it again. There was barely a half meter of snow above the blue ice, so it was impossible to dig a hole. We were lucky enough to find a large boulder with some sort of shelter behind it. With whirlwinds nearly turning us upside down, we managed to build a wall as a windbreak, before digging the tent down. We were all hoping for better weather on the morrow and the chance of climbing Eliassentind. It was named then and there after Odd and also after the highest mountain where he lives in Finnmark. Looking up, it seemed rather steep, but we managed to discover a route along one of the ridges. Some time later we stood on the summit, built a cairn, and photographed ourselves with a self timer, waving the Norwegian flag. It was dead calm on the summit, while down below, and on the way up, the wind was bitter cold. This was our experience on nearly all summits.

At the same time we did the neighbouring mountain, which we named Mount Bård, at the same time. Admittedly it was not as high as Eliassen, but then Bård is not as tall as Odd. After these successful climbs, we were punished next day with bad weather, driving snow and visibility down to nil. The day dragged on interminably and we were bored stiff, lying on our backs gazing at the roof of the tent or dozing off to kill time before our next meal. What was worse, our reading matter was giving out. Luckily the bad weather only lasted one day, and the next dawned brightly with a clear blue sky. Odd and I had been bickering over which route to take on the next peak on which we had decided. Odd got his way, and I trailed behind in a fit of the sulks, while Bård diplomatically trudged along in the middle. Of course we were bound not to see eye to eye in everything. Bård wrote in his diary that I had snapped at Odd. I sometimes felt that they did not want me there at all. With the three of us cooped up together

in a small tent, and thrown on each others' company all day long, conflicts could scarcely be avoided. Everyday things concerned us; everything from the choice of route to the consistency of the soup. On the whole, however, things went well, and our friendship survived. We duly climbed the bone of contention. Once more we were treated to a fantastic downhill run. There were many good ski runs down from our climbs. The slopes were long and suitably steep, often with a sprinkling of newly fallen snow.

We were not quite sure where to go next. There were two possibilities, but here again the terrain did not quite agree with the map. Two mountains seemed to be missing. We chose the peak that looked the most challenging, by the route that seemed most difficult. This turned out to be a happy choice, as when we got a little further up we could see that the other route ended in an icefall 100 metres high.

One evening when the sun was low in the sky, we reached the end of the Humboldt ice stream. The mountain peaks, in crimson evening light, cast long shadows. It was a solemn thought, being the first human beings among all these fantastic mountains. Sokkhornet, a red granite pyramid some 1,500 metres high, dominated the foreground. That evening, none of us were in a hurry to go into the tent. We also saw our first birds, two grey, gull-like creatures who landed close by, inspecting us with studied calm. 'Snowgulls' seemed an appropriate classification.

The Humboldt ice stream is the biggest one to traverse the massif. It debouches a few days'

skiing south of the Novolazarevskaya base. We decided to follow it north, sampling on our way some of the highest and most prominent peaks it had to offer. Sokkhornet was, of course, magnificent, but much too difficult, at any rate for Bård and me, who are skiers above all. In the end we chose Zwieselhogda, the highest summit east of Humboldt. We had not given up Sokkhornet altogether, hoping, eventually, to find an easier way up. We went over to feel the mountain, which was solid as concrete, and rose up several hundred metres perpendicularly straight up from the

steep ski slopes.

ODDEMANN

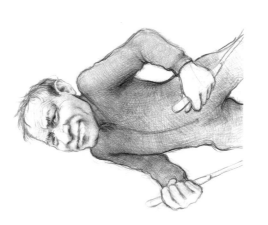

The most exposed areas were nothing but glassy icefields.

glacier. At the foot, we found running water, and were able to slake our thirst properly for the first time in weeks. Odd suggested this would be a great place for package tours, bringing rock climbers to lash themselves to smooth and untouched granite. All that was needed was an airport.

Zwieselhøgda turned out to be a large massif, and it was a long climb to the top. For a long time, we were not even sure whether we had reached the highest point or not. Another summit manifested itself, which might just conceivably have been a few centimetres higher than 'our' summit. To reachit, we would have had to go down - and up again. We could not bear the thought. Instead we went home via the back of Søkkhornet. That dashed all hopes of an easy ascent. On the other hand, as we followed the red granite walls, we were rewarded by yet another fantastic revelation of the power of Nature. At regular intervals, we passed blue and white hanging glaciers shining in the sun, while veils of snow were driven along the mountain flank. Time was getting short, we ought to be moving northwards. It was a wrench having to leave all these wonderful peaks behind. There was so much we had been unable to accomplish, and it was going to be a long time before anyone came this way again.

Down the Humboldt ice stream, we found the warmth about which we had dreamt all the time. Sometimes it was almost too hot even to ski in only underclothes. With only a few days left to go, time passed quickly. There was no longer any hurry. We cast around for something to climb, casually adding a few easy peaks to our bag. For example, there was Haitanna ('The Shark's Tooth') and Eidshaugen. Each peak had its own peculiarities. Haitanna , (the name was Odd's), in no way resembled a shark's tooth. The summit itself consisted of a collection of 'statues' in all shapes and sizes, sand-blasted by the wind. One of Nature's freak creations, which would have been the envy of many a sculptor.

Our last ascent of any importance was Altertavlen. Having grubbed around for a long time trying to find the right way up, we stumbled on Alterduken (the Altar Cloth). Alterduken,

We'd come back if we could.

a steep, snow-covered glacier, made a fitting approach to Altertavlen. We trod carefully, fearing to make holes in it or mar it's pristine freshness. We felt ourselves on holy ground when we finally got to the top and were able to survey the area we had been traversing the last fortnight.

On our way north we encountered several sizeable peaks: Svarthornet, Gråkammen and Hjortehorna. In their dramatic impact, they did not lie far behind Ulvetanna. We also passed Nordvestøya, dotted with spires not unlike those which grace Gaudi's cathedral in Barcelona.

During the last week of our long journey we had a day or two of cloudy weather and snow. This was a change; all in all we had not had more than four or five days of unsettled weather. If anyone feels going south in search of sunbathing, there is a little bit of Norway down here, with can provide plenty of sunshine.

The maps we used were made after the Norwegian Maudheim expedition of 1956-60 had done a triangulation survey on the north side of the mountains. This survey, supplemented by aerial photographs, were the foundation on which these maps were based. They also showed an astronomical survey and triangulation points on Askeladden, a nunatak marked on the way to Novo. We put our faith in typographical errors, hoping instead for a 'gastronomical' point - and set off accordingly with high hopes. All we found at the top was a cairn and an iron bolt. The astronomical station was conspicuous by its absence. On the other hand we actually did find something which might be called gastronomical. On a little knoll there was an old dog sledge with some crates of rancid seal blubber, some tins of butter and a little dried milk. We made out words like 'Christmas hamper' and 'Oslo' so could only conclude that these were the remains of a depot laid by the Norwegian Antarctic Expedition; or dumped before they returned to their base at Norway Station.

The Polar Institute had warned us that the skiing might give out just north of the mountains. In the worst case, we might have uninterrupted blue ice for the last 100-150 km in to

Provisions and dog food from the Norwegian Antarctic Expedition 1956-60.

Novo. We dreaded the idea of having to trudge along on crampons from morning to night, but luckily it turned out to be a false alarm. We did not hit blue ice until we had only 10 km left to go.

The last few days on the way to the Novo base became a simple travelling stage, while the mountains disappeared under the southern horizon. We were obviously approaching civilization, and at regular intervals we saw traces of human activity. Besides the Russian Novolazarevskaya there was a German, (former East German) and an Indian base on the same bare moraine ridge. But nobody had ventured further than the last numataks we had passed.

A thick fog came down on the day we were hoping to reach the Russian base. That day of all days we could have done with proper visibility - just in case we overshot the mark, but there was no difficulty as it turned out. We crossed the track from the base to the airstrip, which was marked empty oil drums every five yards. We rounded the last ridge, and there on the gravel heaps below us, lay our destination. From this distance it resembled Norwegian State Railways' maintenance works for old carriages, which were dotted about the landscape on trestles.

The very last downhill slope presented us with problems. It was steep, icy and covered in spillage from earlier thaws. This (of all times) was when I managed to wreck the sledge - with only ten metres left to go.

As we came closer, the place began to look more like a car breakers' yard with old tractors and engine parts strewn around. Grease-stained Russians welcomed us with open arms. Lena came hurrying along, to embrace each one of us, her eyes full of tears. I do not believe it was the high wind which was causing those tears.

The rest of the expedition had not yet arrived, so we monopolised attention, and were offered all the luxury available: hot showers, ditto meals, sauna, camp beds and vodka galore.

In all, we had made 13 first ascents and travelled almost 550 km across Norwegian territory where human beings had never before set foot. It made us quite proud, and we wondered if the Foreign Office ought to have sponsored us, since we so wholeheartedly upheld Norwegian interests in the area - or at least they might have presented us with a small medal. . . . .

In the Land of the Cairn Builders

Ever since the days of the Vikings we have built cairns on top of the highest mountains. In the Middle Ages people lighted beacons to warn the people of war and unrest. In later days, beacons, or cairns, as they are now called are the sign of a first ascent of a particular mountain. It is a sign to the next comer and the rest of the world, that this mountain has been climbed before, often with a visiting card with the date hidden inside. Today nearly all mountains have been climbed. Tanzania's flag waves from the top of Kilimanjaro, there is an aluminium crucifix on top of Aconcagua, and on top of Mt. McKinley there were three Spaniards. At least there were in 1992, when Odd and I went there. People have been nearly everywhere.

In the Norwegian Touring Association's old year books, we can still read about what it was like being first, building a cairn where nobody had ever been before. In those days the sense of adventure and excitement was overwhelming. The route of William Cecil Slingsby, the English pioneer of climbing in Norway, to the summit of Store Skagastølstind was what we would now call a beginner's route. But at the time Slingsby's partner, Mohn, was sure that Slingsby was going to a certain death. Slingsby himself was nervous and unsure of himself when he left Mohn and climbed to the top alone.

We experienced something of the same sense of adventure and excitement at being first. Even although a helicopter had once landed on Jøkulkyrkja no one had yet been up there on foot. We had to find our own route to the top, without any help from previous climbers. We climbed each mountain by the easiest route, or at any rate, what looked like the easiest route. Ulvetanna was in a class of its own, but also Kinntanna, Gessnertind and Holtanna were real challenges. Some of our 'mountains' were really only small nunataks, but all of them have received a cairn on top, and thereby deserve a place on this list. We were, you see, first where no others had been before us. Welcome to the land of the cairn builders!

First Ascents

In the following list we have used altitudes and positions on the map on page 8-9. Most probably, the only correct altitude is that of Jokulkyrkja, while the remaining peaks are about 20 metres higher than shown. The peaks are listed in inverse order of altitude starting with Norway's Highest Mountain. Most of the mountains have a short standardized description of each peak, while Gessnertind, Habermehltoppen, Kinntanna and Hel have each been more amply treated. Altitudes determined by us are in italics. (The margin of error may be considerable.) We have also used italics where we ourselves named a mountain. Names in parentheses are of purely personal interest. Parentheses also indicate supplementary information. Welcome to the land of the cairn builders!

JØKULKYRKJA (*KONG OLAVS FJELL*)
ALTITUDE: 3148 m.
FIRST ASCENT: 10 January 1994 2100 hrs by Robert Caspersen, Thomas Cosgriff, Odd Eliassen, Jan Åge Gundersen, Trond Hilde, Sjur Nesheim, Erik Skogly Nielsen, Jan Palmers, Carl Emil Petersen, Vebjørn Sand, Bård Stokkan, Jo Toftdahl and Ivar Erik Tollefsen.

HABERMEHLTOPPEN
ALTITUDE: 2945m.
FIRST ASCENT: 13 January 1994 by Trond Hilde.

SANDEGGTIND
ALTITUDE: 3053 m.
FIRST ASCENT: 22 january 1994 by Odd Eliassen, Bård Stokkan and Jo Toftdahl.

GESSNERTIND
ALTITUDE: 3020 m.
FIRST ASCENT: 14 january 1994 by Rubert Caspersen, Jan Åge Gundersen and Sjur Nesheim.

MIKKELSHØ
ALTITUDE: 2641 m.
FIRST ASCENT: 14 January 1994 by Trond Hilde.

ULVETANNA:
ALTITUDE: 2931 m.
FIRST ASCENT: 2 February 1994 by Robert Caspersen, Sjur Nesheim and Ivar Erik Tollefsen.

DRONNINGA (*NINJAS FJELL*)
ALTITUDE: *approx. 2925 m.*
FIRST ASCENT: 31 January 1994 by Odd Eliassen, Bård Stokkan and Jo Toftdahl.

STOKKANTOPPEN
ALTITUDE: 2906 m.
FIRST ASCENT: 22 January 1994 by Odd Eliassen, Bård Stokkan and Jo Toftdahl.

ELIASSEN
ALTITUDE: 2895 m.
FIRST ASCENT: 27 January 1994 by Odd Eliassen, Bård Stokkan and Jo Toftdahl.

GRATISHAUGEN
ALTITUDE: *approx. 2820 m.*
FIRST ASCENT: 30 January 1994 by Odd Eliassen, Bård Stokkan and Jo Toftdahl

Sandeggtind

BÅRDS FJELL
ALTITUDE: 2830 m.
FIRST ASCENT: 27 January 1994 by Odd Eliassen, Bård Stokkan and Jo Toftdahl

ST HANSHAUGEN
ALTITUDE: *approx. 2810 m.*
FIRST ASCENT: 30 January 1994 by Odd Eliassen, Bård Stokkan and Jo Toftdahl.

VESLEBJØRKEN (*JORUNS FJELL*)
ALTITUDE: 2775 m.
FIRST ASCENT: 21 January 1994 by Odd Eliassen, Bård Stokkan and Jo Toftdahl.

KINNTANNA
ALTITUDE: 2724 m.
FIRST ASCENT: 6 February 1994 by Thomas Cosgriff, Jan Åge Gundersen and Trond Hilde

GJERULDSENHØGDA
ALTITUDE: 2640 m.
FIRST ASCENT: 25 January 1994 by Odd Eliassen, Bård Stokkan and Jo Toftdahl.

ALTARTAVLA
ALTITUDE: 2641 m.
FIRST ASCENT: 3 February 1994 by Odd Eliassen, Bård Stokkan og Jo Toftdahl.

MÜLLERKAMMEN (*LOKES TIND*)
ALTITUDE: 2620 m.
FIRST ASCENT: 15 January 1994 by Odd Eliassen, Bård Stokkan and Jo Toftdahl

HOLSTTIND (*HOLTANNA'S NORTH SUMMIT*)
ALTITUDE: 2577 m.
FIRST ASCENT: 6 february 1994 by Robert Caspersen, Sjur Nesheim and Ivar Erik Tollefsen.

MUNDLAUGA
ALTITUDE: 2455 m.
FIRST ASCENT: 19 January 1994 by Ivar Erik Tollefsen.

HEL
ALTITUDE: 2335 m.
FIRST ASCENT: 19 January 1994 by Robert Caspersen and Jan Åge Gundersen.

TUNGESPISSEN
ALTITUDE: 2277 m.
FIRST ASCENT: 15 January 1994 by Erik Skogly Nielsen and Ivar Erik Tollefsen.

PHILIPTANNA
ALTITUDE: 2200 m.
FIRST ASCENT: 15 January 1994 by Erik Skogly Nielsen and Ivar Erik Tollefsen.

HAITANNA
ALTITUDE: *approx. 2010 m.*
FIRST ASCENT: 1 February 1994 by Odd Eliassen, Bård Stokkan and Jo Toftdahl

NINJASKJERET (*THE SOUTHERN NUNATAK IN THE HOLTANNA PASS*)
ALTITUDE: 2000 m.
FIRST ASCENT: 17 January 1994 by Trond Hilde and Ivar Erik Tollefsen.

NICKSKJERET (*THE NORTHERN NUNATAK IN THE HOLTANNA PASS*)
ALTITUDE: 1952 m.
FIRST ASCENT: 17 January 1994 by Trond Hilde and Ivar Erik Tollefsen.

NICKS FJELL
ALTITUDE: 1860 m.
FIRST ASCENT: 1 February 1994 by Odd Eliassen, Bård Stokkan and Jo Toftdahl.

THE SOUTHERN NUNATAK IN THE HOLTANNA PASS
ALTITUDE: approx. 1850 m.
FIRST ASCENT: 21 January 1994 by Robert Caspersen, Sjur Nesheim and Ivar Erik Tollefsen.

ØRNESKJERET
ALTITUDE: approx. 1770 m.
FIRST ASCENT: 17 January 1994 by Trond Hilde and Ivar Erik Tollefsen.

PYRAMIDESKJERET
ALTITUDE: 1687 m.
FIRST ASCENT: 14 January 1994 by Ivar Erik Tollefsen.

TVILLINGHAUGEN
ALTITUDE: approx. 1630 m.
FIRST ASCENT: 14 January 1994 by Ivar Erik Tollefsen.

HÅKONSKJERET
ALTITUDE: approx. 1620 m.
FIRST ASCENT: 2 February 1994 by Vebjørn Sand.

GUDMUNDSKJERET
ALTITUDE: approx. 1610 m.
FIRST ASCENT: 2 February 1994 by Vebjørn Sand.

VESLESKJERET (IN THE CONTINUATION OF FENRISTUNGA)
ALTITUDE: approx. 1570 m.
FIRST ASCENT: 14 January 1994 by Ivar Erik Tollefsen.

SOLSKJERET
ALTITUDE: 1568 m.
FIRST ASCENT: 14 January 1994 by Ivar Erik Tollefsen.

TVILLINGSKJERET
ALTITUDE: 1540 m.
FIRST ASCENT: 2 February 1994 by Trond Hilde and Jan Åge Gundersen.

KIMSKJERET
ALTITUDE: approx. 1560 m.
FIRST ASCENT: 14 January 1994 by Trond Hilde and Erik Skogly Nielsen.

Gessnertind

By Sjur Nesheim

Majestic. Desolate. Standing on top of Jokul-kyrkja we get our first glimpse of Gessnertind. It will take us two days on skis to reach it. North of Gessnertind the icefield runs gently down to the Antarctic Ocean. To the south the land is dominated by steep granite pinnacles.

'Which route are we taking?' The wind tears at the fabric of our tent. We are camped in a long, broad, gap between Gessnertind and Habermehltoppen. Jan Åge, Robert and I make up the team. 'It looks pretty steep on the top wall. Look at that flank of snow just below the summit.' Early tomorrow morning we'll be on our way. The long days are light, polar night and the Midnight Sun are still to come. Our approach is classical in its simplicity, the mountain promising in its strength and power. All-embracing Antarctica.

On the way to the ridge for which we are aiming, the snow is heavy and clinging. It is our first steep climb down here. What is the avalanche danger? We advance carefully. Solidity and homogeneous structure convince us. Ice follows snow. We come face to face with the rock. Yellow granite. Porous. Eroded. Few belays. It will have to be the snow. Two long ropelengths and we are faced with the first of many choices. Take the west ridge? Traverse across the north flank? We choose the latter, trusting that common sense will lead us to the logical route in a multitude of structures, fissures and formations.

Ropelength follows ropelength. Classic alpine mountain climbing. Activity. Ice axe in a groove. Crampons on projecting crystals. Snow packed down hard. Day merges into night. There is dense cloud, but high above the summit. The temperature quickly drops to minus twenty five degrees. It is an all-embracing climbing experience.

We reach our summit, a mighty nunatak in a continent of endless plateaux and un-climbed mountains. Our most pressing problem is how to get down again. But for a short moment we are a few privileged people on this earth. This is our hour. Early next morning, we are approaching the tents. A lone man comes to greet us. Carl Emil, of course. Hot tea from a thermos flask. 'Congratulations! Well done boys.'

Gessnertind

Kinntanna

By Thomas Cosgriff

We had come down from Ulvetanna thoroughly disappointed and demoralized. I'm not sure how Trond had felt about retreating, but I felt terrible. The whole reason I had come to Dronning Maud Land was to climb a big-wall, and now that we had failed, I felt that I had no reason for being here and that the whole trip was a waste. I had quickly forgotten how much fun I'd had on the boat with the Russians, skiing around on the shelf ice with hundreds of penguins chasing after us, the fantastic views from the top of Jokullkyrkja and the fine ski trip back to basecamp. Everything was clouded by my failure on Ulvetanna.

After a few days moping around in basecamp eating cookies and sorting out our heaps of equipment, we finally decided to go for a ski tour up on the Fenriss tongue to see if we could find any peaks which looked easy enough for us to climb. The Russians were due to pick us up in just over one week, so we needed to find a route that could be done quickly and mostly free. We had no time for haul bags, portaledges and lots of technical climbing.

The wild, gargoyled summit of Midgard was the first thing that caught our attention. We managed to climb about three meters up it's loose and ugly rock before we came snivelling down and returned to basecamp. It began to look as though nothing would get climbed in the Fenrisskjeften. After two weeks there, we still hadn't done anything big. Ivar's team seemed to be standing still on the west face of Ulvetanna, and time was running out. I secretly began to like the idea of leaving the area without having climbed a single peak. That we had come so far, tried so hard and had still not managed a single major peak would have been paying a fitting tribute to the most impressive mountain range that I had ever seen. However, such was not to be. The Ulvetanna team began making progress again, and we, becoming more and more hyperactive on our high sugar diet, decided to make one last climbing attempt, this time on the second highest of the Fenriss peaks, Kinntanna.

We had skied around Kinntanna several times during the past weeks, eyeing it for possible routes. The only feasible route we could see went straight up a steep 600 m arete in the middle of the north face. This route looked rotten and blank for long sections, however it did have the advantage of being an extremely direct line to the summit. This would make the descent relatively safe and simple. As we had no time for anything else, we decided to at least try it.

For me, the hardest part of any climb is the approach, particularly if it involves snow and ice. The approach to Kinntanna was my worst nightmare: traversing unroped hundreds of meters across steep hard ice with several large, gaping crevasses below. The others, all from Norway and thus born and raised on such steep and icy terrain, were not the least bit bothered. They cruised up to the base of the rock arete in no time. I however, remembering my first winter outing in Norway when I fractured three vertebra during a hundred meter fall down an ice gully (so that's why crampon toe bails now come with safety straps!...), plodded up the steep bits on all fours. As I was carrying the complete rock rack, I wasn't particularly worried about Trond and Jan Age climbing on without me.

Conditions were perfect for climbing: dry rock, clear skies and not a breath of wind. We began by soloing up an easy low angle ropelength to a large shelf. Above the shelf, the steep angle and dubious looking rock told us that it was time to rope up. Fun but unprotected free climbing up crumbly swiss-cheese rock led up 20 m to a perfect hand crack. Although the crack was nice for getting in protection, we discovered quickly that our hands were much happier holding on to thin, sunny edges than being stuffed into a dark and very cold crack. Back onto the sunny face higher up the climbing got steeper and the rock got worse. Finding good belay anchors in the steep rubble was not an enjoyable challenge!

The next ropelength led up to a sloping snow covered shelf that threatened to spit us out into space when we tottered across with our smooth-soled shoes. A few meters above I made a belay in the only possible place, hanging in the shade, deep in a corner. The contrast in temperature between out on the face and back in the corner was surprisingly large – 20 to 30°C in just a few meters. We all agreed that it was far too cold to free climb up the corner wearing only our friction shoes, and as we had neither the time nor the equipment to climb much technically, we decided to give up for the day and return the next morning when this section would be warmed by the sun. I was not looking forward to the descent down the steep ice, but as my sleeping bag and food were hours away back at basecamp, I had no choice but to follow Trond and Jan Age down.

We were up at four o'clock the next morning to check on the weather. It had snowed a few inches during the night, and Kinntanna was plastered with snow. There was no question of free climbing now, so we took advantage of the situation and slept until noon.

When the sun reappeared about 1 o'clock, we quickly threw our gear into our packs and began the three hour slog back up to the rock.

My paranoia about falling off on the steep ice leading up to the climb was definitely getting better, however I still whimpered across the worse bits and arrived at the base of the climb a half hour after Trond and Jan Age. We had just enough time to jumar up to our high point before the sun disappeared around the corner, leaving us again in the shade. I luckily manager to convince Trond and Jan Age that I was the fastest climber, so while they got to shiver in slings in the shady corner, I got to climb a lovely face pitch leading 60 m up to a sheltered sunny ledge. After fiddling away the next hour nailing and penduluming our way up a steep rotten headwall, it was time to rappel back down the arete and return to basecamp for the night.

The next morning we woke up much later than planned, primarily because of a big dinner the night before which consisted mainly of aquavit and vodka (courtesy of our new Russian friends). After a long, painful approach and strenuous jumar up to our high point, we were confronted with a steep, unprotected slab of rock which looked like it had a few thousand potato-chips glued on to it. Normally the thought of leading off on such a rotten and unprotected face above a big ledge would terrify me, but today I was lucky. I had had lots and lots of aquavit the night before, and as every good climber knows, there is nothing like a bad hangover to make you climb without fear. It turned out that the potato chips were not too crumbly, and after quickly climbing that pitch and the one above, it was time again for the long slog back down to basecamp.

All of our ropes were now hanging on the climb. If we were going to get to the top, we would have to do it in the morning in one last push, taking with us the ropes that we had been using to rappel with every night. Our philosophy on Kinntanna was to free climb while fixing ropes as high as possible, and as soon as all of our ropes were fixed, we would make a push to the summit. Although this approach was slow because we could only freeclimb for the 8 to 10 hours a day that the sun was shining on the face, we saved many days by not having to haul heavy bags stuffed with food, clothing and sleeping bags. Often on big walls more time and energy is spent on hauling than on climbing, and on the rotten flaky rock of Kinntanna, we wanted to avoid hauling at all costs. The downside of this approach was that we were climbing in only our pile jackets and lightweight rock shoes. If anything happened to us which prevented us from getting down quickly, the extreme cold would make the situation very serious. I would have felt much safer if we had been climbing using the big wall approach, such as the guys on Ulvetanna were doing, because than we would always be just a few rappels away from the security and comfort of our portaledges, where a warm sleeping bag was waiting.

We finally managed for once to get up early, although not necessarily because we were so keen go up and start climbing, but more out of practical necessity; the Russians were due to drive us out of the area that night, and we had no intention of missing our ride. We slogged up the ice slope to the rock, thankfully for the last time, and jumared up to our high point 400 m above the snow. On the way, we argued a lot about how many ropes to carry with us to the top. The rough and flaky rock was ideal for getting ropes stuck on. I had terrible visions of being stranded at the top of Kinntanna and watching myself slowly turn blue in the Antarctic night. Trond and Jan Åge thought I was being excessively paranoid when I insisted on climbing with five ropes to the summit. They thought two ropes were enough, but being kind and not wishing to argue too much, they carried the extra ropes.

The climbing to the summit was just like it had been on all the other days; loose and unprotected. When I was leading up the last, rotten ropelength to the top, I thought about how lucky I was to have climbed for 20 years, and also about how much my perspectives on climbing had changed. When I was young, I thought climbing was exhilarating and challenging because of the danger it entailed. I'd often climbed completely out of control, and only shear luck prevented me from getting seriously hurt. Now I am exhilarated for the opposite reason: when the climbing gets hazardous, I feel in control of the situation and I know what I can and cannot do. I tend to climb extremely conservatively now, placing ridiculously large amounts of protection when I can, and when I can't, I use experience to get through the long runouts unharmed.

I started up the final crack leading 15 meters to the summit. As I saw the sky through the backside of the crack, I realized that Kinntanna's summit was shaped like a giant and very thin axe blade. After crawling up onto the 1 meter wide summit ridge, I held out a rock at arms length and dropped it off the back side of the mountain. I counted 12 seconds watching it fall before I lost sight of it. What a wild place to be! Trond and Jan Åge soon joined me on the edge, as stunned as I was by our tremendous position. We

The Molar / Jan Åge and Trond just below the summit.

took turns having our pictures taken balancing on the tiny summit, where the giant axe blade narrows to a little pinnacle 40 x 80 cm wide. After a perfect half hour of sightseeing, we put slings around the pinnacle and carefully began rappelling off.

Habermehltoppen

By Trond Hilde

When it was decided that only a three man party consisting of Jan Age, Sjur and Robert were to climb Gessnertind, I packed my rucksack and went off together with Thomas to climb Habermehltoppen. Nearly 3,000 m. high, it is a steep snow ridge ending in a knife-edge summit ridge.

From the camp, three or four hundred metres west of the glacier flowing from Gessnertind, we ski'd directly south along Kyrkjedalshalsen towards Habermehltoppen. From the glacier, at an altitude of about 1,800 m., there was a relatively steep snow slope towards the beginning of the ridge. Great blisters meant that Thomas decided to turn as soon as he put on his crampons, and tried climbing on front points in the steep snow and ice. From the saddle, there was a fine view of Gessnertind to the north. To the west were parts of the fantastic ridge running down from Jokulkyrkja towards Saurneset

and far to the east I saw Fenriskjeften with its brutal fangs. The saddle was a steep and exposed snow ridge; the slightest mistake, and I would have plummeted to the bottom. I went slowly along the knife-edge ridge towards the summit. The snow ridge turn to a narrow, sharp arête of bare rock with perpendicular flanks, partly lined with loose snow.

Varying rock made climbing difficult. Without ropes and protection, and equipped only with an ice axe, I stopped a few metres below the summit. I sat and savoured the feeling of being alone, and the view from one of the highest vantage points in Queen Maud Land. An icy wind imposed a limit to how long the appreciation could last, and once the summit was scaled, the magic would be broken. The return went well, and I granted myself a good rest, sheltered by some stones. When I was almost down, I could see the boys on Gessnertind. They had passed the glacier, and were up on the summit we had previously defined as the pyramid. They would scarcely be down again before the small hours. I was back in the camp between 6-7 o'clock in the evening.

The following day, I climbed the unnamed summit next to Habermehl, and called it Mikkelsho, after my son Mikkel.

We stuck our first rope on our fifth rappel, in a place where the rock didn't look like it should cause any problems. On the next rappel we stuck another rope, and I began to feel justified in my paranoia. After a little calculation, we concluded that if we tied all of our remaining ropes together into a single line, the line would be long enough to reach the top of the first pitch. From there it would be relatively easy to downclimb unroped to our ledge above the snow. The economic implications of abandoning seven expensive ropes up on the wall seemed inconsequential when we felt the wind begin to blow and saw the clouds building up. We wanted down! We tied the ropes together and began rappelling.

A few hours later, surrounded by warmth and comfort, drinking beer and eating fried chicken in the big orange Russian Winnabago, I realized with satisfaction that my Antarctic climbing career was over. I hate the cold.

On the summit!

Topography of the route up to Kinntanna.

A Close Shave on Hel...

By Jan-Åge Gundersen

She lay like a temptress in the shadow of Ulvetanna. The north side of the mountain we had chosen, which was almost visible from Base Camp, consisted of a high, vertical wall, several hundred metres high. Out skiing the day before, we had discovered from a distance that the south side was less steep, and that a snow slope reached half way up the mountainside. Robert and I were in the mood for a nice day out, so we set off, hoping to reach the top.

At the start a long stretch of blue ice impeded our progress, so that we had to resort to crampons. It was not steep, but demanding enough. We zigzagged between bottomless

crevasses. This was no place to stumble. Another hundred metres or so brought us to a less windswept area, where the snow had settled like a blanket to conceal faults in the ice. We roped up, wending our way up the shoulder until we came to a ridge which eventually became so steep that the snow would not hold. We took a break, changing our footgear and dumping unnecessary weight.

Apart from one or two ticklish sections to begin with, it was easy enough using running belays. Further up we came upon a marvellous stretch of smooth rock which continued upwards in a steep upper wall. I was impatient with Robert, convinced that he was purposely dawdling. We took turns leading, and even although the climbing became harder, it did not take us long to get to the top. We broke loose some slabs of rock and built a cairn, took the requisite pictures of the view and made ready to start on the descent.

Robert fixed the rappel anchor, clipped in the 100-metre rope in the carabiner and prepared to rappel. Owing to a twist in the rope he was unable to tie a knot in the dangling rope ends. After he had lowered himself down some way, he stopped on a shelf and tied the

Blue ice on the way to Hel.

knot which was to prevent him from rappelling off the end of the rope. He rappelled all the way down and I could feel the rope swinging as he tried to retrieve a sling we had placed on the way up. I was hanging beside the upper belay, keeping an eye on it, when I heard noises which should not have been there, noises which cut me to the marrow like an electric shock. Looking down, I could see that Robert had fallen down the mountainside. In falling, he had first hit his back on an outcrop, where he had actually managed to twist his body round, before continuing down the wall, half falling, half running. In the space of those seconds Robert was at the mercy of the gods. For one terrible moment it looked as though Hel, the old Norse Goddess of Death, would claim him for her own. But Norn, the Goddess of Fate thought otherwise. A shelf, two metres long and one metre wide stopped the fateful drama. He got to his feet apparently unhurt, swung round, stooped slightly and then shrieked in a voice trembling with desperation, anger and fright: 'I nearly died!' Half a metre to the right of where he had landed, the mountain fell several hundred metres down into the abyss. Robert was lucky. The knot on the end of the rope had loosened, and he had shot downwards in uncontrolled flight.

When we were on the summit, Robert had changed into the smooth inner boots which went with his plastic boots, making it possible to slide over the rock. Had he been wearing his rockshoes when he fell, he would have braked suddenly, fallen over, and been unable to stop when he hit the shelf. Being able to keep on his feet probably saved his life. As it was, the only damage was a few bruises and a lacerated thumb. Shaking like a leaf I retrieved the rope, tying a huge knot at the end. I then rappelled down and reached the shelf after climbing down Robert's homemade switchback. We bandaged Robert's thumb, before continuing our way down. Robert had scarcely managed to ease himself over the edge, when, with his back to the abyss he saw a white Antarctic petrel rise from the summit and circle steadily upwards. A religious veil covered his face, and he explained that this was his benefactor, Norn, manifesting herself in the guise of a bird, to give us strength for the descent.

We eventually got down by lowering Robert past the most difficult passages while he, at the same time, fixed running belays to protect me. To save time, and also because the rope might catch on the rock-face, causing more drama, we decided not to rappel. After a nerve-racking descent, we reached the equipment we had dumped on the divide

between snow and rock. Then it was across the blue ice and through the gap once more.

On the way to Base Camp it dawned on me that this nerve-racking episode had given me something new to think about. I imagined Robert falling, a foot or so more to the right and crashing down onto the blue ice, and saw myself skiing into Base Camp alone, as the messenger of death. I was glad that Robert was alive, and was overcome by an intense feeling that what we were doing was insane. For the space of one short hour I really believed that as far as I was concerned my climbing career was over, and that the rest of my time in Antarctica would be given over to philosophical discussions with Vebjørn, relieved by a little occasional skiing. The movie reel of Robert falling past that shelf was repeated again and again, presumably until it wore out. For down at Base Camp, the event itself was displaced by the story-telling art for which the excitement was fertile soil, and Robert and I were most concerned to convince the others that it really was the goddess of death, Hel, that we had climbed.

The author on the way to the summit of Hel.

Postscript

At the end of June, 1994, Vebjørn Sand and Ivar Tollefsen spent some time in Athos, working on the text and paintings from Queen Maud Land. The strong will and friendliness of the monks made a great impression on the two Norwegians.

At the foot of Mount Athos, for the past thousand years, Greek orthodox monks have dedicated their lives to work and prayer. Among historians and scholars all over the world, the monastic community on the peninsula in the north of the Aegean Sea is considered to be one of the most well preserved and living cultural treasures of our time. From its foundation in 969 AD. down to the present, very little has changed. In spite of fire and pillage, the monastery still contains literature and paintings of incalculable value. Women are not allowed inside, and men are only admitted on short visits, for which special permission must be obtained.

'Let's go monk hunting,' said Ivar. We were stretched out on a mountain ledge in Athos. Far below us the Aegean Sea shone blue, and the sun was at its hottest. Four months earlier there had been other black creatures in our zoom lenses - penguins. Their abode was the enormous ice shelf which marks the beginning of Antarctica. Monks, however, were a more difficult quarry than penguins. After several embarrassing misses, Ivar and I agreed that next time a lonely recluse came along, I was to take aim and Ivar would shoot.

Greek monks have erected a chapel on the top of Athos, an altar closer to Heaven. This serves to give us some idea of the religious conception of mountains in ancient times: the place on earth where one was closest to heaven. Down the ages, mountains and hill tops have been the scene of initiation into insight and wisdom. The mythology of ancient cultures was closely bound up with mountains. On those inaccessible heights, the Gods had their abode. Everyone has heard of the Greeks' Mount Olympus. But also in the Judaeo-Christian tradition, the mountains have had their significance, not as a dwelling of the Almighty, but as the place where Man can come into contact with Him. Here, offerings were made, and altars built; and chapels too.

Abraham went up on to the high ground to offer up his son, Isaac. Moses received the Ten Commandments on Mount Sinai. In the New Testament we hear of The Sermon on the Mount, the Ascension of Christ into Heaven. It is said of Jesus that he went up into the mountains to pray.

During the Middle Ages, mountains became associated with fear and darkness. Here in Norway, trolls and fearsome giants roamed the mountains. The Pagan Gods had become the powers of evil, which men must fear, and Nature was merely an idol.

In more recent times, it is in the year 1335 that we first hear of anyone climbing a mountain in the modern sense of the word. The Italian renaissance humanist, Petrarch, and his brother climbed Mont Ventoux in Provence. All Petrarch wanted was to look at the view and rejoice in Creation as befitted a true son of the Renaissance. But the ascent gave Petrarch great agony of soul: 'I love that which it is not mine to love!' he lamented. For when he had reached the summit, and having with him a copy of Augustine's 'Confessions' his glance happened to fall on the words: 'And the sons of men go forth and worship the high mountains, and thereby do forsake themselves'.

The people of the Middle Ages were taught to seek God within the depths of their own souls. Worshipping Nature, however beautiful it may be (Augustine called Creation 'God's carmen - His song) only served to lead people astray. Worshipping Him with our hearts and minds is more pleasing to the Lord our God. Petrarch felt as though he had been rebuked.

Our forefathers regarded the mountains with fear and trepidation. Middle Age man's fear and superstition was the result of theologists' and also Augustine's condemnation of belief in ancient pagan gods. This reflects a perception of both the divine and the destructive forces inherent in mankind. In Petrarch veneration had its renaissance, not in the worship of the gods, but in the joyful appreciation of Nature. He saw mountains as altars. His attitude was not one of indifference. He was no ordinary tourist though he was the precursor of modern tourism. He observed the forces torn between veneration and fear, the exalted and and the gloomy.

Long before Petrarch, in the time of David, the Book of Psalms says: 'Who shall ascend into the hill of the Lord? or who shall stand in his holy place? He that hath clean hands, and a pure heart, and a pure heart; who hath not lifted up his soul unto vanity, nor sworn deceitfully.' He, who in David's time, walked on the mountains without having purified his soul, was guilty of blasphemous behaviour. Perhaps it is this which lies underneath the angst in popular superstition?

Mountains have lost their mythic significance for modern man. We have forgotten the words of the psalm. Mountains are the object neither of fear or prayer, but tourism.

Of our thirteen man strong expedition from Norway, there probably was not one of us who gave David's psalm so much as a thought. We who grew up with building society houses, top-of-the-pops and disc jockeys. And on Monday, 10 January 1994 at 21.00 hours, our whole assembled party could plant the Norwegian flag on the summit of Norway's Highest Mountain!

Modern man's attitude to Nature and mountains is characterized by superficiality and not intensity, conquest and not profundity. This is the result of a long historical and spiritual process; we are no longer subject to the might of Nature, we can choose whether we will fear, love or totally disregard her. The great advances of modern times have been accomplished through each single one of us: through individuality. Naked man's individuality and power of perception, facing as yet unbowed a world which no longer has any tangible meaning, but which is waiting in the shadows, daring us to find a new significance - and bring it forth once more into the light. As the Norwegian poet, Henrik Wergeland puts it: 'Each man is a lord on earth, each man a priest to God.' If you so wish, you also can be a priest on a high mountain. We no longer believe it to be the prerogative of initiates and anointed priests.

When we first came to the mountain world of Queen Maud Land, I felt that we still had a remnant of reverence and awe. We were the first human beings there, on a journey of exploration in a mythic and enigmatic land.

But we came also as conquerors, invaders from the modern world with our sponsor pennants ready for every peak which was attained. Where our forefathers would have built altars and sacrificial places, we built our cairns.

In my mind's eye I can still see the great icy spaces, the ice shelf, and far in the distance - the mountains of Queen Maud Land, rising up like everlasting cathedrals in the wilderness of white. Against a pure light surface and sky, lonely rocks rise up, and I think of gothic church spires. Then I realize why, in ancient times, before men changed gods, mountains were holy ground. We had come to the most inaccessible, the coldest, least hospitable, yet perhaps the most distinctively beautiful place in the whole world: The land we know least about - the last continent on earth.

In Queen Maud Land, which is just about as far away as you can get, it is easy to think about incomprehensible things, the land which belongs to the realm of dreams - where anyone who will, can be a king or a queen.

Vebjørn Sand
Athos, 21 June 1994

The Expedition would like to thank...

Our aim was to climb the steep and difficult mountains of the world's coldest and most windswept continent, far from civilization and in regions where human beings had never been before. We achieved our aim well within the allotted time, with more than 30 first ascents, of which the ascent of Ulvetanna was probably the most hazardous route ever to be attempted in the Antarctic. We took 15,000 pictures, developing hundreds of these at our own Base Camp before sending them to Aftenposten via satellite. We filmed under extreme circumstances and temperatures and were nevertheless able to send live TV images home to Norway. We ran our own post office at Base Camp. All this was only made possible thanks to the co-operation and dedication of many separate individuals and Norway's leading industrial concerns. We thank you all for a wonderful trip and an experience we shall never forget.

Main co-operating partners:
ABB Nera AS (Satellite Communications)
Cap Computas (Data Consultants)
CPC Foods AS (Knorr Soups)
Expertkjeden & Sony Norge (Electronics and consultancy)

Aftenposten AS
Allweek AS (Boxer shorts)
Alpina Norge AS (Alpina BC Skiboots)
American Express Co. AS (Credit cards and travel insurance)
American Express Reisebyrå AS (Travel Agency)
Berema AS (Honda electricity generators)
Urmaker Bjerke AS (Rolex Explorer II watches)
Cannor AS (Canon cameras and accessories)
Carl Emil AS (Paper for books and calendars)
Finn Clausen AS (Personal planning consultants)
Crispi Norge AS (Crispi mountain skis & Telemark boots, and Morotto skis.)
Duracell Norge AS (Batteries)
E-post (E mail)
Forsvarets batterilaboratorium
Forsvarets Forskningsinstitutt
AS Freia (Chocolate)
G-Sport AS (Sports equipment)
Heatpac AS (Personal heaters)
Hellanor AS (Coleman burners)
Helly Hansen AS (Underwear & outer clothing)
Helsport AS (Sleeping bags & tents)
Hjemmet Mortensen Bokforlag AS
Hufa Luefabrikk AS (Winter headgear)
Ingolf Kristiansen (Shoemaker)
Inmarsat
Kunsthuset AS
Livewire Digital Ltd.

Lufthansa German Airlines AS (Airline)
M2 eiendomsmegling AS (Estate agents)
Mack's Ølbryggeri AS (U-nik sports drink)
Maxware AS (Software for electronic mail)
Midelfart & Co. (Piz Buin suntan cream)
Mjørud AS
Nefab AS (Transport crates)
Norsk Polar Institutt
Norwegian Telecom AS (Satellite communications)
AS Nopal (Dried foods, vitamin supplements)
Ota AS/Jensen 6 Co. AS (Crüsli breakfast cereal)
Jens Otterbech (Norwegian Ambassador to South Africa)
Norwegian Post Office, postage stamp division.
Rieber & Søn AS (Maryland Cookies biscuits)
Rottefella AS (Ski bindings)
Russian Antarctic Expedition
Scan Alpine Services AS Scan Alp (DMM climbing harnesses, carabiners and protection equipment, Edelrid ropes, harnesses and helmets)
Scan Optik AS (Cebe sunglasses)
Shipmate Norge AS (Panasonic GPS satellite navigator)
Siemen's AS (Solar panels)
Siemen's Nixdorf Informasjonssystemer AS (Environment-friendly notebook)
Skandinavisk Høyfjellsutstyr AS
Ski Silketrykk AS
Sony Norge (Video cameras & electronics)
Stibolt Norge Ski AS (Berghaus rucksacks and gaiters, Scarpa expedition boots and rockshoes, Sigg drinking and fuel flasks, Insul-a-Mat groundsheets)
Stokkan Agentur (Environment-friendly ashtrays)
Swix Sport AS (Ski wax, ski sticks and ear muffs.
Telepost Communication AS (Electronic mail)
TV2
Utenriksdepartementet (The Norwegian Foreign Ministry)

AS Vinmonopolet (Lysholm Linie Aquavit)
Vinylfabrikken AS (Woollen gloves and mittens)
VHF Communication AS (Radio communications)
Arne Winther/AM-Lab (Photo services)
Zürich Insurance
Østlandsmiljø AS (Fibreglass sacks)
Østlands-Postens printing works

Angela Amoroso
Susan Barr
Roger Bilden
Christer Bonde
Per Brustad
David Durkan
Per Christian Dæhlien
Trond Eiken
Mikal Eriksen
Hans Christian Erlandsen
Marko Franken
Jan Erling Haugland
Sigurd G. Helle
Thomas Hertzberg
Roland Huntford
Ralph Høibakk
Tina Jørgensen
Valery Lukin
Bjørn Lytskjold
Sjur Mordre
Lena Nikoleva
Cathrine Reed
Barbara Robole
Morten Rostrup
Jorun and Øystein Stokkan
Erik Wallter Tollefsen
Wiggo Wideroe
Tristan Wood

Queen Maud Land

We have been able to visit a fairyland, the like of which is scarcely to be found, and would like to thank all those who have bought one or more of these portfolios for the contribution they have made to the expedition.

Aftenposten AS
Alpina Norge AS
American Express Company AS
Jan William Andersen
Cap Computas AS
Carl Emil AS
Finn Clausen AS
CPC Foods AS
Crispi Norge AS
David Durkan(ScanAlp)
Eilag AS
Mette Franck
Åse og Jørgen Fredriksen
Fagernes Sport AS
Petter Gjølstad
Hjemmet Mortensen bokforlag AS
Turid Manshaus
Mjorud AS
Nopal AS
Prank&Torgersen AS
Even Ronvik
Scan Optik AS
Siemens Nixdorf Informasjonssystemer AS
Sony Norge
Haakon Sæter
Ivar Tangen
Zürich Forsikring

VIEW TOWARDS JØKULKYRKJA

The lithographic portfolio, Queen Maud Land, is a high quality work printed by Grafisk Stentrykk AS, executed under the supervision of Kjell Johansen, assisted by Jan Martin Ulvåg. The artist, who worked directly on the stone, has also supervised the whole production process. The technique is lithography, the edition limited to 175 -one hundred and seventy-five - copies. In addition there are some Épreuves d'artiste. The pictures are printed on French handmade paper - Velin Cuve BFK Rives blanc 270 grammes. The pictures are printed in various colours - which means using the same number of stones and the same number of times through the press.

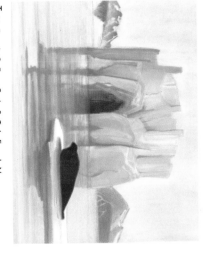

FENRISKJEFTEN

THE ICE CASTLE IN MAGDALENAFJORDEN

ULVETANNA

Orig. trykk vedlagt

Winter darkness has once more descended over the Jaws of the Wolf.

Gusts of wind hurl stones and ice blocks through the air and the thermometer shows an incomprehensible

60 degrees below zero. While the driving snow collects like white froth round the pointed fangs of the Wolf,

Fenriskjeften's petrified animal kingdom wakens to life once more.